LESLEY VAN STAVEREN
SPEAKER ● CONNECTOR ● INNOVATOR

Be Your Own Hero

8 STEPS TO TRANSFORM YOUR LIFE

Copyright © 2020 by Lesley Van Staveren

All rights reserved. Apart from fair dealing for the purposes of study, research, criticism or review as permitted under the Copyright Act, no part of this publication may be reproduced, distributed or transmitted in any form or by any means without prior written permission.

The information in this book is not intended to replace professional medical or psychological advice. The content is based upon the author's personal and professional experiences, opinions and qualifications.

Lesley Van Staveren: www.lesleyvanstaveren.com.au

Cover design by Chris Hildenbrand
Typeset in Palatino Linotype 9/12pt & Quicksand Medium 12/22pt
Printed and bound in Australia by IngramSpark
Prepared for publication by Dr Juliette Lachemeier @ The Erudite Pen

 A catalogue record for this book is available from the National Library of Australia

Be Your Own Hero: Lesley Van Staveren – 1st ed.
ISBN 978-0-6489900-0-0

Dedication

To my children, may you flow through life living with full hearts, having faith in yourselves and your abilities to achieve anything you choose to commit your lives to.

May you be kind, gracious and know that you have greatness within.

To the father of my children, I am so grateful for the journey we have been on as it has blessed me with beautiful learnings and experiences, which makes me who I am today.

To my readers, may this spark the confidence you need to take control of aspects of your life that are outside your comfort zone. May you appreciate how spectacular you are and love the uniqueness of your whole being.

Embrace life; this isn't a rehearsal. Make it count in every way possible, for you and for the greater good.

Lesley Van Staveren

Contents

Preface 1
The 'Knight in Shining Armour' Myth 5
Have You Got Your Own Back? 35
Rock the Boat 53
Perceived Fear of Inadequacy 73
Understanding Your Body's Responses 105
Owning Your Personal Power 135
Owning Your Mistakes 155
Self-Acceptance 177

Preface

This is a revolutionary book if you need a wake-up call to stop waiting for someone else to save you or make your life better. It is a reminder that you control your own destiny.

Throughout the following chapters, you will be expertly guided on how to take ownership of your life choices from business and finances to relationships.

Be Your Own Hero is a powerhouse in your corner. It will reassure you that you can trust your intuition, get educated and find the courage to make big decisions that have life-changing outcomes. This will empower you to feel self-worth, draw boundaries and never again give your choices and control away.

There is a saying, 'If you are trying to please everyone, you please no one.' When you understand and respect yourself, you'll realise that deep inside you actually have more to give when you don't compromise your values.

Nobody is coming to save you. When you realise that, you take your power back. The key is to gain strength in your own capabilities while keeping an open heart.

The fascinating thing is that once you start to have faith in yourself and respect your own opinions, you can begin to build the most important relationship of all: the one with yourself.

I have created this book for you to work through, a bit like a workbook. I encourage you to reflect on each chapter's questions and take time to write your responses.

This book is also delivered as a life-coaching program so I can guide you through your transformation, helping you to own the strength that resides within you.

Every chapter focuses on a different theme, detailed in this infographic:

I do share parts of my own life experience with you; however, ultimately, this is a book about you and owning your personal power.

Wishing you all the very best on your journey to *Be Your Own Hero*,

The 'Knight in Shining Armour' Myth

How many of you are hanging on by a thread just accepting what life throws at you while coasting along on autopilot?

I never for a moment thought I would be approaching forty and starting my whole life over. But you know what, that's on me. I recognise that I played a part in this outcome, which has become a vital part of my processing and healing. I am now in a place where I accept that I wasn't my best self for many years. By not honouring the best parts of me or letting them come through, this showed up in various areas of my life.

When your world flips on its head, you can feel like all is lost. However, this could be just the beginning of something new and wonderful. My favourite sentence right now is, 'It is what it is.'

If you are in a difficult situation personally or where another party is involved, the most powerful gift you can give yourself is to compassionately understand, for example, that no one ever intends to end up losing their business, relationship or house. Why would they? But this could also represent a series of events that might have been rectified much earlier if you were to take ownership of and be aware of your life as a whole. You need to listen to your intuition and believe in your ability to handle all areas of your life.

Having faith in someone else isn't a bad thing. Unfortunately, problems can arise when faith is confused with not wanting to disrupt a relationship just to keep the peace, letting things trickle along as they are because it seems like the easier option.

It goes back to the old saying, 'What is easy in life is not always the right path.'

Women, particularly, grow up hearing stories about knights in shining armour and living happily ever after. And who hasn't heard that if you work hard enough, you will be rewarded. Does that happen in every case? No, absolutely not.

But what if you were taught to perceive things differently? To accept that you need to take control and let the cards fall where they may. What if you had undeniable faith in yourself, your ability to handle all situations and your right to speak up and say no when things don't feel right? What if you were educated about the true reality of life, which very rarely involves knights in shining armour? Then you empower yourself with an internal peace that grounds you in a sense of security that is yours and yours alone.

I encourage you not to wait for the 'Big Break' or 'The One' to make your life what you dreamed it would be. You need to take ownership of your own life and *be your own hero*. Then you know anything else that comes into your world on top of this is a bonus.

When you are not your own hero, one day you may have a rude awakening that everyone else is making decisions about your life without you even realising it. Sounds crazy, right? But the sad fact is there is always a payoff later down the line if you don't take responsibility for yourself and your life.

I know from experience that when I get into the monotony of daily life, I can fall into bad habits. And so can you. Then one day you wake up and realise you gave too much of yourself away. The key throughout life is to have balance and self-respect, while also being grounded in yourself, your values and your self-worth.

You must understand how valuable you are and be responsible for yourself and your actions. Remember this though: You must keep expanding your heart, not contracting it. Part of the tapestry of life is being able to lean into relationships with each person contributing to the greater good. I am not discouraging relationships in this book; I encourage you to be in a position of internal love and acceptance to then give yourself and the person you are with your best self.

A beautiful and balanced place to be in a relationship is when you have equal respect for each other, and both create the space for one another to thrive and feel loved and appreciated.

── Be Your Own Hero ──

> Let's now explore this in a way that is personal to you. I'd like you to pause, breathe deeply and take a moment to write down your answers to these questions:

As a child, who did you seek approval from?

In relationships, in what areas do you rely on someone else to take charge? In what areas do you seek reassurance? (It could be about your finances, what you're wearing, how you look, where you are allowed to go, who you can associate with).

Lesley Van Staveren

At work, home or when socialising, how well do you communicate your ideas or opinions, especially when they differ to others'?

Do you have faith that your friends have your best interests at heart? Do you have absolute confidence they are with you through thick and thin?

Be Your Own Hero

If someone has a different opinion to you, how do you react? Are you open to listening and respecting their views or do you feel they should come around to your way of thinking?

Do you read every contract you sign and understand the full consequences of the worst-case scenario?

Lesley Van Staveren

Are you in control of your finances? If not, who is?

Are you happy with your reflection in the mirror?

Do you know what you stand for?

Be Your Own Hero

Where have you held back in life for fear of what others may think?

Do you have full trust in your own abilities to get you to where you want to be? If not, why not?

Lesley Van Staveren

Do you know your own worth?

Let's take a closer look at these questions and what your answers might mean in relation to being your own hero:

As a child, who did you seek approval from?

This is such an important question! How you sought approval in your formative years is a behaviour that stays with you—until you become aware of it.

For example, did you need some significant other to approve of your appearance before going out? What common sentences did you hear? Were you compared to anyone else? This can stay with you.

Growing up, I was a challenging child, full of self-expression. Unfortunately, back in the early 1980s, people weren't sure what that meant and saw it as a matter for concern, so I got taken to doctors to find out what was 'wrong' with me. I would often hear, 'Why can't you be more like your sister?'

My beautiful sister played by the rules and was the well-behaved one out of the two of us, so my parents knew how to deal with her. Ironically, as we grew up and reached our adult years, we realised that we actually felt the same about each other! We had both compared ourselves to each other throughout our early years. I was convinced she was the favourite as she was the good one, and she believed I was the favourite because of the attention I received.

From my level of understanding at the time, I grew up thinking I wasn't good enough in comparison to everyone else, so I felt small and worthless. But this was a story I created based on limited information as a child; it took a lot of work to realise this was not the case. Once realised, I went back to basics and started appreciating my own value as a human being.

The majority of us have developed a need for external approval. It's necessary to acknowledge this so we can free ourselves from it. I do understand that the need for approval comes from our basic, built-in survival system and the need to be included in a tribe in order to survive. But humans have evolved since then. Our approval needs to come from within; we need to fully accept who we are and what we are about.

Self-acceptance will help us to stop judging and comparing ourselves to anyone else. We all have our own way of being, and accepting ourselves doesn't mean that we don't want to grow, just that we accept our starting point with kindness. This acceptance can then nurture further growth. This enables us to free ourselves and step into our own rhythm, building relationships where we can appreciate each other for our unique gifts without worrying about how we measure up.

In relationships, in what areas do you rely on someone else to take charge? In what areas do you seek reassurance? (It could be your finances, what you're wearing, how you look, where you are allowed to go, who you can associate with).

It can be so easy to allow another person to take control of certain parts of our life, because, after all, it's a partnership. A factor to consider is what part is being controlled and whether our values are in line. The responsibility for finances is commonly taken on by one partner or the other, due to sharing a life. However, the challenge comes when we have different values on how money should be managed or have very different financial habits.

Ultimately we need to be educated on where our money is, how it's being spent and all financial plans for the future. I encourage everyone to get expert advice on this. It doesn't mean we have to be cold and calculating when it comes to money, but we need to take ownership and have the final say in anything connected to our security in life and our future.

But let's get back to you. Where else in your relationships do you allow someone else to do what you have the ability to do? It's great to receive love and help from others; this is a very necessary part of life. But you should be aware of why you are letting someone else make decisions for anything in your life, or doing things for you that you think you can't. This is where the problem lies. You are giving your power away when you do this. When you start to explore all the areas in your home or work life that you gladly let someone else handle, ask yourself if this is because you don't think you can either do it or don't have confidence in your own opinion. This is a great place to start to find balance; it also shows you if you are avoiding things. Who knows, reflecting on this could perhaps uncover strengths you didn't even know you had.

At work, home or when socialising, how well do you communicate your ideas or opinions, especially when they differ to others'?

What came up for you when I asked the question about communicating an idea or opinion? This relates to all areas of life. Do you have confidence in what you have to say? Or do you keep quiet because you think you may sound stupid or that no one will be interested?

Your opinions matter. If you don't stand up for yourself and say what you feel, who else will? By having the internal confidence to say what you feel or share an idea you have, it allows you to live your truth and not bottle up what you want to say. Holding in your voice can result in frustration and resentment, and it doesn't allow you to be free. If you don't speak up because you are worried about what the response will be, think what that means about the person you are speaking to? If someone does not respect what you have to say, you need to ask why and what that means for you.

People in your corner will always hear you out and give you respect even if they disagree. Different opinions are necessary and enrich our lives; it's how we respond to them that counts.

The key factor is how you communicate what you have to say. Are you personally clear on your beliefs? What do you feel strongly about and where does that come from? You should spend time gaining as much knowledge as you can in areas that you are passionate about. There's so much information in this world and it's accessible at any moment. However, when researching into an area, ensure that it is factual as there is also a lot of misinformation out there. Identify where or who the information has come from as bias can and does exist in the writer's own beliefs and experiences. That's natural. It's important, therefore, to find reliable sources or verified material.

If you have seen something occur that you disagree with, or you have a cause that you are putting your time and energy into, you can project yourself with confidence, not arrogance or disrespect. You can also create the greatest impact through compassion and empathy. This can be in a situation that you disagree with in life, where the other party may genuinely not know any different. You then have an incredible opportunity to allow another person to see from a different perspective.

Ironically, in my early years I used to be terrified of speaking up or having any attention drawn to me for fear of looking or sounding stupid. Eventually I realised that it was all in my head. I denied myself the opportunity of having a voice because I didn't have internal confidence and I didn't believe in my worth.

Next time you have the chance to use your voice, will you? What steps can you take to help you feel more comfortable communicating your thoughts? For example: If you have a meeting coming up, can you do research and breathing exercises to get yourself in the best mental space so you're prepared to use that voice?

Do you have faith that your friends have your best interests at heart? Do you have absolute confidence they are with you through thick and thin?

What thoughts came to you around friendship? Your inner circle should be behind you all the way, championing you along, cushioning your falls in the low moments of life and celebrating your wins.

I'm blessed with several people in my circle that I know hands down have my back. It is them that I confide in because they won't jump in the mud with me in the difficult times. They stay above the line and ask me questions so that I can process my thoughts and come to the right conclusion about what is best for me and my life.

It's taken a long time for me to get to this point. I think we can all relate to finding out in the worst way when someone doesn't have our back and lets us down. But that's just the way things are, and it doesn't mean we need to hold on to disappointment. If we have had a rude awakening and found out we have been stabbed in the back, it may take time to process. We aren't meant to get along with everyone and we also have to explore our part in what has occurred. We each have responsibility for every outcome. The skill is to find it, acknowledge it and own it.

It's also okay to let people go from our life that bring us down or make us feel bad. We can trust our gut feeling as that is where the answers lie.

Lesley Van Staveren

If someone has a different opinion to you, how do you react? Are you open to listening and respecting their views or do you feel they should come around to your way of thinking?

What revelations came to you when exploring your response to different opinions? Do you dig your heels in and argue your point? Or do you take the time to be quiet and truly in the other person's space even if you disagree?

This is a great indication of your awareness around accepting yourself and others. Let's face it, who says your truth and opinions are more valid than another person's? For them, they also fully believe in what they are saying just as you do.

It is having confidence in what you believe, and the knowledge that you don't have to be 'right' that can give you peace inside. Having the skill to listen and walk away when you need to is a magnificent way to conserve energy and also respect yourself and others.

This does not mean you should accept things you know are absolutely wrong, or allow someone else to do or say things that bring you down. There is a big difference between a healthy debate and allowing another person to insult, degrade or manipulate you. You must stand up for yourself when another person is working to coerce you into doing something you don't want to. That is your integrity and self-respect coming into play, and it is essential that this is able to rise to the surface.

Do you read every contract you sign and understand the full consequences of the worst-case scenario?

This goes for your personal life and in business. Read the fine print and never sign anything by just going with the flow. You should never allow anyone, even if they are trustworthy, to tell you to sign on the dotted line without knowing what you're getting into. It's vital to be aware of the worst-case scenario even though it may never happen. But if it does, you will have given yourself the gift of knowing how to respond and what actions to take. This minimises being caught off guard.

Read the fine print every single time as there may be hidden fees, services or personal liability. This is something I have learnt the hard way because I trusted those around me and didn't have my own back. Other people may have the best intentions and trust is certainly not a bad thing as it's a vital part of building fulfilling relationships. What I ask though, is that you trust yourself to know what you are signing no matter what it is, and to understand all the associated aspects. You have the skill and ability to be savvy in this area, so you need to trust yourself.

It can be so easy if you are in a happy state or excited to sign a piece of paper and only think of the good outcomes. But you must be pragmatic and know all implications because ultimately it is your life that will be impacted.

Are you in control of your finances? If not, who is?

Is it you? Or is it your spouse? Or have you engaged someone to manage your money?

Do you look after your own finances, and do you feel in control and knowledgeable? Or is it overwhelming? To be independent and secure means getting educated on budgeting and cash flow, both personally and professionally. If you are not someone who enjoys numbers, think of it a different way and consider what this knowledge gives you. It allows you to be secure, plan for your future and avoid surprises further down the line.

I have learnt this the hard way. I'm an intelligent woman, but circumstances in my life resulted in me giving a lot of decisions away that I should have been responsible for. I own this, because at the end of the day, by not choosing to take full control of all decisions, I essentially chose to give my power away.

Don't learn the hard way. I recommend reviewing all income and expenses regularly and getting a regular advisor. Read books about money, take a short course and get educated. This is your life we are talking about.

By tuning your brain in this direction, knowledge will flow through each decision you make. Then slowly but surely you will gain the financial security and acumen to create the foundations you hope for.

If the person in control of your finances is not you, you need to ensure you are aware and involved in any decisions made. If you feel you do not have enough information or understanding to make decisions in this area, this is the time to take ownership and get educated as it is your life and long-term security that is important here. You have the ability to continue to learn more every day.

Remember this: Financial health gives you options and freedom.

Lesley Van Staveren

Are you happy with your reflection in the mirror?

How did this question make you feel?

It's not just about the physical aspect, although that is a major consideration that I will get to. It's about you as a person. When you really look at yourself, are you satisfied with the person you are? None of us are perfect, we make mistakes and will continue to do so. But do you live true to yourself and do the right thing whenever you can? Have you put something off in your life that you have always wanted to do?

In my mid to late teens I was incredibly disruptive. I avoided going to school, hung around the streets with groups of my friends and started smoking and drinking alcohol far too young. I learned so much in those years, and I found that even though I wasn't on the right path at the time, I followed my gut instinct and made a choice to get a job and follow a career path. I knew the person I was and that my behaviours weren't in line with my character. I am a very open, soft soul, although I am not scared to stand up and speak out when I need to.

Is the person in the reflection the one who is living up to their full potential?

Let's move on to physical appearance. How easy is it to be dissatisfied with how you look? Too often I hear people say they wish they were skinnier, prettier, curvier, taller, shorter, had smoother hair, curlier hair etc. The list goes on.

It doesn't matter about how you look; it's how you feel and your personal acceptance of the extraordinary person that you are. You don't need anyone else's approval, or to ever compare yourself against anyone else. I used to feel like the short, ugly one with an odd deep voice, then I woke up and realised what I have is unique. I'm one in seven billion . . . and so are you.

Learn to love everything physical about yourself. For too long has the tall poppy syndrome prevailed. Or being taught to not be big-headed or 'full of ourselves', but that's not what appreciation and gratitude for your physical self is. It is pure acceptance and love, which then allows you to remove barriers such as comparing yourself to others. This again allows you to appreciate others as well as yourself for everyone's unique beauty. Being content with who you are allows for living from your heart and getting out of survival mode.

Do you know what you stand for?

Lesley Van Staveren

We live in an awakened era and will often hear people talking about their purpose or their 'WHY'. These are key aspects to bring into who we are. If we don't know what we stand for or what drives us, we are not living our own life but rather one that is expected of us.

But back to you: Knowing what drives you enables you to bring things into your life that resonate and keep you living a life that is true to you. It may not always be perfect or easy, but life isn't supposed to be that way. You are thrown hurdles to jump over so you can keep learning the lessons you need to. And if you keep having the same problems or challenges show up, you need to consider whether or not you have learnt the lesson.

For me, I have absolute clarity about what drives me: It's caring for the planet we live on and preserving this spectacular world for future generations to come.

This clarity allows me to work in fields that contribute to my main purpose; for example, I have worked in the plastic industry for ten years now. I co-founded a recycled manufacturing facility as I believe we need to continue to find ways to re-use the resources we already have in existence. I also founded a not-for-profit organisation enabling others to come together and make a bigger, more positive environmental impact by considering each action we make in our daily life from our consumption, what we buy and where it ends up. I believe we are all able to make a difference as an individual and as a collective.

I have since moved on from these roles and now coach others on interpersonal communication and internal strength. This still aligns with my ultimate goal in life of having an inspiring, positive impact on people and the planet.

The abovementioned ultimate goal led me to my desire to enable more people to feel content within themselves. The more people are able to step out of the daily struggle that life can be, the more they can look outward and care for their surroundings and beyond. It all starts with us, as individuals, having confidence in ourselves and being clear on what we stand for.

When I am going through rough moments, of which I certainly am as I write this book, I am also at peace, knowing all I do is done with integrity and for a greater positive impact. I am where I am supposed to be at this moment in time.

I believe we should all spend some time getting to know our inner selves, what motivates us and keeps us moving forward. Or perhaps getting to know what causes inspire us the most and pull at our heart strings. It's important to follow this path and explore what resonates with us the most and how we could get involved.

Where have you held back in life for fear of what others may think?

When you have internal doubt in your own abilities, fear creeps in. This is why you have to be your own hero and back yourself.

In my school years I would be terrified of getting asked a question in class for fear of sounding stupid and for what people thought of me. This resulted in me shrinking into myself to the point I would avoid going to school. I didn't think I was enough, or that I had the ability to do well, so I stopped trying.

I made that choice. If I'd had more faith in myself as a teenager, I would have made very different decisions, but it is what it is, and you know what, I don't regret this. It was a learning curve in my life and, ironically, I am now a public speaker and thrive at the chance to share my knowledge that may be of value to others.

Everyone is scared of something, and quite often in life we may make decisions to hold back for fear of what others think, but whose life does this make a difference to? Ours, not theirs. It may sound harsh, but other people don't think about us in the way that we worry about. People are going to make judgements and form their own opinions no matter we do; it's not something we can control, and neither should we try to. That's a lot of wasted energy that we could instead direct towards our own growth.

We will work on fears a little further into the book.

Do you have full trust in your own abilities to get you to where you want to be? If not, why not?

What feeling came up when I asked the question about trusting in your own abilities? Was there a long pause? Uncertainty? Or perhaps absolute certainty about possible strengths and weaknesses?

Doubting your capabilities can hold you back from learning new skills or perhaps going for the job you really want. So can carrying past criticisms as this stops you from trying. But let me ask this: How can you make positive decisions in your life if you don't trust yourself?

This is where you might hand over choices about your life to someone else because it feels easier.

Self-doubt can also affect your home life. Do you put up with circumstances that you are not happy with and stay where you are for fear of your ability to cope alone? Guess what, you can cope. If you start to trust the knowledge you have and your ability to develop new skills, you can continue to make decisions that you can be sure of. They may not always have the outcome you hoped, but isn't that part of life?

Reflecting on my life, I can see so many times where I doubted myself, and the consequence of this is that I gave my power away. We need to trust in ourselves and what we are capable of. When we do this, no matter the outcome of the decisions we make, we can be at peace that we made the best choice for ourselves with the information we had at the time.

Do you know your own worth?

Having a deep internal confidence in yourself impacts your life across the board. Knowing with clarity what your strengths are enables you to speak up and believe in what you say. It also allows you to be clear on your weaknesses and brush up on those. Have you ever held back because you have an underlying belief that you are not good enough or haven't spoken up because you feel someone else knows better? I ask that you pause for a moment right now. Yes, put the book down and write down when you have held back and why.

Trusting that you have value to contribute, that you have a voice and an opinion worth hearing allows you to be free and live a life true to yourself.

I spent so many years thinking everyone else's opinion was worth more than mine. As I mentioned, I grew up thinking I was insignificant and felt less than everyone else around me. But I recognise that was my perception at the time, and an inaccurate one at that. What I ask you to consider is that every single one of us is unique and has a wealth of knowledge, with our own experiences and beliefs to share. Everyone has a right to have their voice heard and has something of worth to give, and this includes you!

It's now time to get clear on your worth and what you have to offer, appreciate yourself and what you are capable of and know it, deep in your heart. You don't need approval from any-

Lesley Van Staveren

one else but yourself. Here and now, you are enough.

Have You Got Your Own Back?

When you are going through periods of personal growth and becoming more self-savvy, please bear in mind you should not exclude others or close yourself off. You need to have love and appreciation for yourself as well as for others. When you expand your heart space, you grow in strength. Having a deep respect for your own abilities and worth actually allows you to more freely connect with those around you from a place of strength, as opposed to a place of doubt. That is a beautiful place to be.

Loving yourself does not mean you think you are better than anyone else. No one is any more or less than anyone else. You have a right to appreciate who you are.

So, ask yourself this: Have you got your own back? What this means is speaking positively to yourself, rolling with the punches and being proud of yourself no matter what. You could probably tell me your friends who are undeniably in your corner, but are you personally on that list?

When I make mention of accepting yourself as you are, you need to ensure you're using positive language about what you accept. It's not helpful to beat yourself up or accept what you believe are negatives about yourself. For example, you may have a belief that there is something you cannot do because you don't have the skill, so you just accept it. NO, absolutely not! This is an aspect you have to look into further if it's stopping you from doing something you really want to.

You will probably have your friends' or family's back, championing them and always being there for them no matter what. You need to do this for yourself too.

Why? There are so many reasons that I'll get into. Here's one example: If you don't believe in yourself, you may continue to unknowingly allow others to make choices for you either in big or small ways. Every time you allow someone else to do something for you that you could have done yourself, you are then choosing to give part of your life ownership away.

The challenge is when you believe someone else knows better than you what is right for you. But they are making decisions based on their own experiences and values, not yours. This may not necessarily right for you. I believe you must all develop inner confidence and trust in speaking up for what you know is right for you and your life.

Be Your Own Hero

> Let's now explore this in a way that is personal to you. I'd like you to pause, breathe deeply and take a moment to write down your answers to these questions:

Are you proud of yourself? Why or why not?

Lesley Van Staveren

Do you doubt yourself and keep from speaking up, even when you know with certainty that you don't agree with something? Reflect on why this is.

Do you wish you were different to how you are? How so and why?

What do you tell yourself if you make what you perceive to be a mistake?

Are you willing to feel 'negative' emotions? If not, why not?

Let's now take a closer look at these questions and what your answers might mean in relation to being your own hero:

Are you proud of yourself? Why or why not?

If you are proud of yourself, fantastic. Pride is a platform upon which inner confidence can thrive, and it links directly to self-worth. Think about all the areas this inner confidence benefits you and reward yourself for this.

If you didn't know how to answer this question, I urge you to ask yourself why not? Perhaps explore what you are not proud of and then work to resolve that. This gives you a starting point.

Is it possible you don't believe that others will be impressed by what you're proud of? If so, it doesn't matter. This is not about them, it's about you, so write it down anyway!

Are you doing anything that you feel deep inside is wrong? If so, these are some serious alarm bells. Stop and think what it is and start identifying the steps to correct this and get back on track.

There could be a variety of reasons where this could stem from, some of which will go back to how and where you seek approval. You need to be kind to yourself. Give yourself a pat on the back for your achievements.

Here's why you should be proud of yourself: You have come so far and overcome every challenge you have come up against. You are still standing, right? Acknowledge when you have had difficulties and look at the fact you have moved past them. Try to avoid pinning your pride on gaining material possessions as this is all surface level. Sure, it may feel nice for a bit when you have the things you like; however, this is not fulfilling in an internal sense.

Look at the skills you have developed throughout your lifetime. When you think about it I'm pretty sure there's more there than you realise.

You have made other people smile and contributed to the world around you. This doesn't have to mean grand gestures. Simply existing and being your unique self has made a difference in the world and to someone in your life.

When you can be proud of where you are, no matter what point you are at in life, it gives you the energy to do more.

You may be at a low point reading this. If you are, as hard as this may sound, you need to accept where you are. Be proud of what you have achieved in life, what you know and what you are capable of. Hold your head high and know you are one step closer to being where you want to be. Being proud of who you are and what you can handle is what will carry you through, because you know in your heart you can do this.

If you are at a high point, reward yourself. Recognise and acknowledge what you did to get here and note the skills you applied and what you learned.

Do you doubt yourself and keep from speaking up, even when you know with certainty that you don't agree with something? Reflect on why this is.

I touched upon this question in chapter one, but would like to explore it further here. Did this question bring an image or past experience to your mind?

What are you accepting that you know is wrong, and how does this affect you? This comes back to being able to trust yourself and back your own opinion and feelings. If you disagree with something, the gift of having confidence to speak up is a powerful skill. Yes, there is the saying, 'Pick your battles' and this is certainly a point to bear in mind. However, there are moments in your life that I'm pretty sure you thought of straight away. Moments where you kept quiet because you either worried about sounding silly, may have been scared of the consequences or didn't feel it was your place to speak up.

This may be at home or in the workplace. At work, have you disagreed about something in a meeting, or how something is done, and not voiced that you have a differing view in case no one listens? As I mentioned previously, I have done that in the past. When I was younger, I had less confidence in myself and didn't back myself enough. It turned out, further down the line, that my view of how things should have been done were actually very sound and logical.

So I encourage you to back yourself. It is very likely yours is an opinion that is valid, worth hearing and gives more context and knowledge for team decisions to be made from.

Or how about personally, in a relationship or friendship? Have you have been treated in a way that didn't sit well with you? Speaking up and calling attention to it sets the tone that you are worth more and sets the standard of what behaviour you will accept. Each of us deserves to be treated and spoken to with respect.

This also applies if you see something happening that you disagree with. By having the confidence to call out bad behaviour, there is a lot that can be improved in this world. With each of us looking out for each other and calling out the wrongs, it helps someone else who may not have the strength to at that moment in time.

Do you wish you were different to how you are? How so and why?

Have you ever wished you were slimmer, smarter, prettier, stronger, healthier or had different circumstances? The list of how we wish we were different is often extensive. We have each experienced these types of thoughts, and it's so easy to do so, especially in our low moments.

I would often think I wasn't intelligent enough, pretty enough and was plain and irrelevant. But that was an incorrect perception that I allowed to grow in my head over many years. None of this is true, but it was me who had to accept and own that and stop getting in my own way.

Here's the thing: If you consistently wish to be different from who you are or where you are, or if you don't acknowledge yourself and your circumstances, you are taking away your power to do anything about it.

Self-acceptance of who you are and your life circumstances is the most powerful skill you can master. It gives you the ability to appreciate everything you have in the moment and to look at what you need to do to get to where you want to be. Accepting your moment in time allows you to keep your mindset strong and know with certainty you will achieve the outcome you want.

It is a lot harder to strive forward with your head held high if you are in a place of denial.

On the personal side, I think many of us would have experienced a moment of wishing we were like another person. Don't forget though, the person whose lifestyle or looks you wish for most likely has exactly the same feelings. It's part of human nature; we have these little insecurities pop up and often desire what we haven't got.

Appreciate and respect others for who they are and be happy for them, their achievements and what they have. Then give yourself the same courtesy. Respect yourself for who you are, how you look and what your own unique skill sets are.

Lesley Van Staveren

What do you tell yourself if you make what you perceive to be a mistake? Why?

How you talk to yourself sets the tone for what you will accept in life. When you make a mistake, how harsh are you? Do you criticise yourself or are you kind and able to identify what the lesson has been?

It's so easy to allow a stream of negative self-talk in our minds. In the past, I would actually look in the mirror and be disappointed with who looked back. I had an opinion that I was irrelevant, stupid and not capable or deserving of success or love.

It's very easy to allow negative talk to circle through our minds, particularly if cruel things have been said to us in our younger years or in bad relationships. But, you know what? It's possible to acknowledge this and start fine-tuning what we tell ourselves.

If you are someone struggling with negative self-talk, the first step is to actually realise it. It may be an ingrained habit and just your way of existing through life, and you don't realise you have control over it.

The next time a negative thought pops into your head, I ask that you acknowledge it and actually note it down. Then start to write all of the most common points you say about yourself that don't make you feel that great.

Next I ask that you break this down and recognise where these words come from. Do they genuinely come from you? Or are you echoing what you have heard someone say to you in your past that you have absorbed into the way you see yourself?

I want you to retune your thinking so it aligns with what you actually feel about yourself. Write down what you believe to be true about all your positives. Humans unfortunately have a negative bias. We naturally focus on the negative as it's kept us alive; however, this means we can hear a thousand great things then focus on the one bad thing. Focusing on the positive takes practice, but you can do it.

The ability to catch your negative self-talk is what can propel you to stretch yourself further and be willing to keep trying until you get the result you want. This is honing your resilience skills. If you haven't achieved the results you want the first time and are in the habit of negative self-talk, you are less likely to try again. Ask yourself this though: What if you changed how you view a 'mistake'? What if you viewed it as just the first step to learning what you need to? I wholeheartedly believe in the saying, 'There's no failure, only validated learning.'

I also believe there are great things about all of us, and we need to believe this too. We deserve it.

Are you willing to feel 'negative' emotions? If not, why not?

How often are we programmed that happiness is the most important emotion and we must feel this all the time? Let's face it, happiness is amazing, of course it is, and why wouldn't we want to aim for that feeling?

But let me ask you this: If you were happy all the time, would you really appreciate it?

It's all the other emotions that make life so rich. These emotions enrich your connections with others; they also help you to relate to others and feel compassion for and supportive of someone else's struggles.

So-called 'negative' emotions are ones that give you a deep understanding of yourself. They allow you to see how you act in daily life, and how you treat others or yourself when you are angry, sad, heartbroken or fearful. Obviously, the list goes on, but you get my point.

Understanding how you react and allowing yourself to feel all emotions without resenting the harder feelings gives you the ability to process, acknowledge and accept what is happening in the moment. It's not until you get hit with a curveball do you realise just how much you can handle and how capable you are.

The times of loss and heartbreak are the times that have led to some of the world's greatest love songs or breakthroughs. Moments of frustration and reaching the end of the line have birthed history-making innovations.

I'm not saying you have to change the world in moments of struggle. What I do ask is that you develop the ability to see who you are through the hard times and take the time to let the feelings flow. Be kind to yourself and recognise who you are as you move through it. This is a big ask, but that's the point. It's not meant to be easy, and that's where the gift to yourself is.

This gift is being able to accept this is where you are meant to be at this point in time. It allows you to reach the next chapter of your life, which helps you to keep getting up and pushing forward every day.

It is when you deny feelings and push them down because they hurt too much that will cause a long-term build up. Accepting pain, hurt, anger or grief is what allows you to process each emotion, allowing yourself to feel it even though it hurts. If you blame another person for how you feel, get clear on why and ensure you do seek help to unravel what is happening in your mind. Understand that by issuing any blame, you are taking away your ability to own your feelings and come to terms with them.

Once you are clear on what you are experiencing and why, this then gives you the tools to action a way to resolve it in a healthy way.

I recommend being conscious of movement while you are experiencing difficult circumstances—get outside, go for a walk or bike ride. Connect with nature. These are all really important actions to keep your body and mind in a positive state to process emotions. Likewise, exercise releases chemicals like endorphins and serotonin that can improve your current mood.

Ensure you are eating well, getting sleep and seeking specialist guidance if you are experiencing a difficult time.

For my first question, I asked you to write down the ways you are proud of yourself. This is because I know for a fact there are multiple reasons, and I ask that you see just how many aspects there are about yourself that you should celebrate.

Rock the Boat

Yes, you read that right... I want you to rock the boat! You see, those of us with different perspectives are often told not to challenge the status quo or disrupt the way things are because the systems that are in place work. But do they?

There are so many challenges and issues throughout the world: racism, hate, greed, homelessness, drug abuse, domestic violence, gender inequality, human trafficking, starvation and profit over peace and sustainability of our planet.

All of these issues exist, and they need a shake-up. They need people to speak up with their knowledge, with their education, with their opinions and with their experience and passion. However, all of these challenges are big issues, and they will require far greater action from all of us pulling together than just one person.

There are thousands of other injustices happening every single day, and this is the world we've grown up in, where we're seen as the odd one out or different or wrong if we dare to question the way things are.

There is a very specific reason that I'm starting this chapter at the societal level. I wish to convey that what we accept as we get swept into the monotony of life are the systems that are in place, our education, where we live, processes, the fabric of society at every single level that has come from a long history of people dictating the way that things should be.

Don't get me wrong, we need leaders and people to propose ways forward. This gives us a framework to work and thrive within, and people need this certainty in their lives. But the challenge is do we question these time-honoured ways of living and allow things to carry on as they are because it feels easier that way?

Sometimes disrupting the way things are, challenging the status quo or speaking up might feel too hard, but is it? Allow me to challenge your way of thinking just for a moment. By living in a world where we are conditioned not to rock the boat, is it possible we become conditioned to applying this standard way of life into a way of being, just accepting the way things are? Should we continue to do what is easy in each area of our life for fear of what may happen if we don't? Easy does not equal right.

Sometimes the hardest things in life are the most rewarding, or the right thing to do. So, you can stand your ground, speak out and be passionate about what you believe in. I believe you all have the strength to call out bad behaviours and speak up when you see something happening that you feel deep down is wrong.

My advice to you is that when it comes to your way of life in the home, in the workplace, wherever it is: Use. Your. Voice! You are given a voice for a very specific purpose and this is why, from right at the beginning of this book, I talk about knowing what you stand for and knowing where your approval comes from.

It is being secure, deep down inside, that really allows you to stand in your own power, be true to your beliefs and project what you feel.

Lesley Van Staveren

This is also where setting boundaries comes into play, and I'll come to that.

So rock the boat, just do it with kindness and don't rock it so hard on your individual journey that you rock people out who are also on the same journey. Be respectful of other people and their beliefs and their opinions because they each have very valid points and feelings about what they're communicating.

That's the beautiful thing about human nature; we all have different beliefs and different values. Life is about expressing these in a harmonious way that doesn't disrespect others. Of course, there are obviously exceptions to this rule. If you see someone else being mistreated, acts of violence against others, racism, or things being pushed away that you do need to speak up for, absolutely rock the boat.

We have a lot that we need to work through as a society. My personal passion is the environment. Everything I do comes back to that place, and if people are more at peace with themselves, the more they will care about others around them. Furthermore, they'll care about the world they live in and want to create a strong impact in a sustainable world. So, yes, stand up and speak out.

Be Your Own Hero

Let's now explore this in a way that is personal to you. I'd like you to again pause, breathe deeply and take a moment to write down your answers to these questions:

Is your intimate relationship based on mutual respect or have you allowed parts of yourself to disappear because you are scared of what will happen if you change how things are?

Are you a people pleaser? Why, or why not?

Lesley Van Staveren

Do you agree with how things are done in your workplace? If not, do you speak up?

Have you ever seen someone treat someone else badly and not spoken up? If not, why not?

What have you sacrificed in your life because you were worried about how someone else may react? Was the sacrifice worth it?

Do you feel heard by others when you voice your opinion? If not, please reflect on this.

Let's again take a closer look at these questions and what your answers might mean in relation to being your own hero:

Is your intimate relationship based on mutual respect or have you allowed parts of yourself to disappear because you are scared of what will happen if you change how things are?

When you're in a partnership, or any kind of relationship, it is very easy to allow someone else to do something for you because it takes away extra weight or an extra workload off your shoulders.

It's natural that if any area of your life can be made easier to reduce stress or overwhelm, you say yes. However, this is where mutual respect and strong foundations in a relationship are key. If you are not complete in yourself, confident in your self-worth and very aware of your own capabilities, you can give parts of yourself away over time without even realising it.

To coexist in a really beautiful space, both you and your partner need to be independent and complete in yourselves, and be responsible for your own happiness. You don't rely on the other person to make you feel grounded or content. That has to come from you and you alone.

If you do get to that point where you have struggled, or you have allowed other areas of your life to be controlled by someone else, it doesn't necessarily mean you are weak. Some of the strongest people experience this because it can happen over a long period of time. For example, I am a very strong, independent woman, but in past relationships, I allowed a lot of elements of my life to be out of my control due to a variety of circumstances. But again, that is on me, no one else.

Losing control of your life can start off as really small things, such as letting your other half take the bins out every week because you don't want to. They might start being in the kitchen more and taking control of the meals because you're tired at the end of the day. Perhaps in business, you don't like doing accounts, so you let them handle it.

When you give away parts of yourself, in whatever form that may be, it's an exchange of value and time. Every time you give a piece of yourself away, it will show up and you might possibly have to pay for it further on down the line. Whatever is hard for you to do right now, I encourage you to look at it, look at where your resistance is coming from and face it head on.

A person may be very genuine in trying to help you, and how wonderful is that when you can coexist in a harmonious relationship! Just ensure you know where their intention is coming from and where that may play out down the line.

Things may start off innocently with offers of help. However, years down the line you may find yourself with no control of your finances, business, who you go out with, what you wear, social occasions etc. Next thing you know, you're stuck and left wondering how you can step out in the world alone.

If you do find yourself in this position, remember that you are never alone. This is when you need to have your internal strength, confidence and faith in what you are capable of. Know that you have the courage to take ownership of your life. Because if you don't, someone else will.

Are you a people pleaser? Why, or why not?

It's great to make others happy. I am a self-confessed ex-people pleaser. I would absolutely put myself out there and say yes if someone

Be Your Own Hero

needed something from me. I want to do right by other people. Why wouldn't I? That's a beautiful thing about being human, right?

But the personal impact of being a people pleaser is being unable to rock the boat. It is easier to just say yes than stand in our authenticity. But this means we're not looking after ourselves. We're not setting boundaries. So what came up for you with the question: Are you a people pleaser? Did you think, 'Oh, yes! But I need to say "no" more.'

Saying no is not a bad thing and people respect it when you communicate that in an assertive way. You don't have to be aggressive when you decline a request of your time.

People really respect it when someone does say, 'No, I just can't do it at that time.' This assertion means you are comfortable in setting your boundaries. If you keep saying yes to everything and everyone, you're again giving a piece of yourself away and not saving anything for yourself. One thing to consider is if you do always say yes, what does that mean for the way 'no' makes you feel?

Why don't you say 'no' more often? Are you worried about how people may perceive you or are you worried about rejection? Are you worried about failure? How does the word 'no' make you feel?

I humbly ask you to bear this in mind: If you are trying to please everyone, you don't please anyone, especially not your own wellbeing and your own life.

Moving forward, I recommend you begin listening to your gut. When you don't want to do something or it doesn't feel right, say 'no'. See how that feels. You can still express a 'no' and be respectful at the same time.

Do you agree with how things are done in your workplace? If not, do you speak up?

As I mentioned at the start of this chapter, there are a lot of external factors to bear in mind when challenging the status quo.

You might not agree with the way things are done in the workplace for a variety of reasons. You think of better processes or have better ideas. Communicate these with respect because you want people to embrace your input when you speak up. It could be about the way people in the business are treated. It could be that you see more efficient ways of doing things. It could be that someone with a different strength could step up, or even yourself. Maybe you are capable of more.

If, for example, you see something that could be done better, think about how you wish to communicate this. What could that mean for others involved? What could it mean for those who have been responsible for decisions and management in the past? My recommendation is to approach them and perhaps have a private conversation first.

You may have a role that isn't utilising your skills to their full potential, or maybe you feel you've been looked over for a promotion or opportunity. What I ask is that you do speak up, verbalise it, note it down. When you hold feelings and opinions down, frustration can build.

It's best to be very clear on why you want to raise a change, what the outcome will be, who else it may affect, and the benefit. What's the positive outcome?

Why specifically do you think things aren't working? Can you demonstrate how it could be done better, including what the final result will be?

Being transparent and deeply considerate, while bringing the appropriate parties into the conversation, is a really positive way to go about recommending change.

Lesley Van Staveren

Have you ever seen someone treat someone else badly and not spoken up? If not, why not?

How did that question make you feel? Did you have an image come up in your mind that you recalled and thought, 'I should have said something.' I'm pretty sure that we've all seen things happen throughout our lives that didn't make sense or weren't okay.

It may have been perfectly innocent. It may have been that we all have bad days and don't always speak to each other kindly. We don't. We're human. But there are certain times when it's not acceptable, where we may have seen bullying occur and were too scared to speak up in case some of the attention shifted onto us. It may even be bullying in the workplace. It may be a social occasion where someone has degraded someone else or derisively used those off-handed jokes.

And this is the thing: Rocking the boat doesn't always have to mean upsetting people or causing problems. By approaching situations from a place of calmness, there's a lot that can be resolved and dealt with in a positive way, especially when we enable others to think.

So what is it that came up for you? I'm actually going to ask you to think a little bit deeper about what you could have done differently and why you didn't speak up. I know for me, in my younger years (even in my early twenties) I might've seemed confident, but I really struggled with so much self-doubt. I didn't speak up because I was scared of the outcome. That is natural.

But back to you. When you're thinking about something that happened in the past, I want you to note it down. What could you have done differently and why? What do you think the result would have been? Because as I say, and as we all know, sometimes the hardest thing to do is the right thing.

It might be in the workplace when seeing how someone's treating a colleague. Imagine how much better we can each be by respectfully standing up and saying, 'No, I don't agree with that. That's not okay and this is why.' Just be prepared that that person also has their own values and their own experiences from where they've come from. Their perspective may not be in alignment with yours at all. But if you feel it appropriate to speak up, don't let this hold you back. Maybe you'll be the one who opens their mind to a new way of looking at things.

Often we don't speak up because we're afraid of conflict, but what does that mean for you and how you process differences of opinion?

Through respecting different perspectives and understanding different beliefs, it is possible to come to a place of agreement in a lot of circumstances. However, to do this takes the skill of 'pausing' and truly listening to the other person.

I say to you: The next time you see bad behaviour, challenge yourself to stand up and speak up. Call it out.

This may not suit everyone as we all have varying natures and ways of addressing situations. If you are concerned to speak out or if it is not safe, you may wish to reach out to the person who was impacted negatively and check that they're okay and supported.

What have you sacrificed in your life because you were worried about how someone else may react? Was the sacrifice worth it?

For me, I don't think I've ever felt enough and that may be a common thing for a number of you reading this book.

We women tend to give away our power to other people because of lack of confidence in our own abilities and self-worth. In my life, I've given up my voice in some areas of business, and that is something I'm working on now. I didn't want to speak up because I was scared of how it would impact my home life. But again, often when you give something away that is a part of your life or allow someone else to take control, it may come up further on down the line.

Have you sacrificed financial control? Perhaps your spouse manages all the bills in your household or specifies what you're allowed to spend. Perhaps it's parenting, where their opinion or their ability to verbalise it is stronger than yours. How does that impact the family unit and your own personal mental health?

Does it get in the way of being able to establish a solid routine for the kids and a stable environment? Do you rely on approval from that other person to feel good? Do you need permission to go out?

Do you allow their perception of you to be stronger than your perception of yourself? This comes back to being really strong in yourself and knowing what you believe in and what you want in life. Because every single area that you give up and don't speak up for fear of how someone else might react, well, that's an issue.

Ask yourself why you are worried about the reaction. What do you think the reaction might be? What does that look like on the other side and what does that mean for the way things are? If a person in your life reacts negatively to something you want or to your feelings, beliefs or goals, what does that mean long term?

Let me remind you of this now: Every single person has the right to speak up, to be heard and to be respected when they express an opinion or want to take ownership of their life. If someone does not want you to take ownership of any aspect that relates to you, I encourage you to ask why.

Do you feel heard by others when you voice your opinion? If not, please reflect on this.

It's interesting when you start developing awareness of both individual and group behaviours. Imagine a big dinner party where everyone's chatting. You have the loud characters, the extroverts that are the centre of attention. They are vocal and express themselves, and then you have the quieter individuals, sitting there waiting for their turn to talk. Sometimes that time doesn't come, but they don't want to speak up because they're worried if they do, they still will just be spoken over.

It's a very, very interesting thing where that fear comes from. As I say, we each have our challenges and the background that laid down the foundations for who we are. The people that are very comfortable with speaking up often appear confident and make their opinions known. But perhaps they have their own insecurities that they are working through. By the same token, they may be in a very good spot where they absolutely have full belief in what they're saying and how to communicate that across and get the right message out there. Everyone is different, and we can never judge.

But what about for you? Do you feel like you're heard? Are you scared of raising your voice in groups? Where does that fear come from?

Is it literally that you are scared of speaking in front of people or are you unsure of your opinion and what you have to say? Because they are very different things.

If you're scared of speaking in front of people and being looked at and receiving any attention, then I encourage you to explore that, look at why.

Lesley Van Staveren

If you can't express yourself, you will feel bottled up and not heard, and then frustration builds. If it's more the case that you are content as you are, that's wonderful. However, it's not ideal if you have something to say but you're not quite sure where to start. Pay attention to what doesn't feel right. Do you have a feeling or a reaction but are not sure where it comes from?

I recommend you start paying attention to your body. When you get an uncomfortable feeling, I ask that you pause and think what's actually stirred it up. What doesn't feel right to you? You have the right to be heard. You are entitled to voice your opinion and to make yourself known. You have a voice and your opinion has worth and value. Own it and know it deep inside your heart.

Perceived Fear of Inadequacy

Perceived fear is a fascinating subject. While there are some very real fears in this world, equally there are a substantial number of barriers that we put in place for ourselves.

It is natural to have some fears and to have boundaries in place. This protects us in life and ensures we consider the worst-case scenario. We need to logically process the consequences of any actions we take or decisions we make.

However, the problem is when those fears become a debilitating undercurrent and restrict you from realising and owning your full potential. Each one of you is capable of greatness if you allow yourself to see it, believe it and feel it.

A number of these barriers can be a self-fulfilling prophecy if you don't challenge them and weigh up all aspects. You then need to have the courage to take the required leaps, being confident that you can handle whatever the outcome is.

I'd like you to now tune into yourself. Can you recall a time where you have surprised yourself by handling a tough situation? Or perhaps you have taken on a task that you didn't think you had the ability to do?

What if you could take a step further into your own self-belief and simply know you are capable of handling all elements of your life by yourself?

——— Be Your Own Hero ———

> The following are some of the likely self-imposed fears that we all tend to suffer from, and I ask you to consider each fear from three different angles:

Be Your Own Hero

You are scared of what others will think of you.

Is this fear relevant to you and how has it impacted your life?

What could you achieve if this was not a concern to you?

What will you change about how you perceive this barrier?

Lesley Van Staveren

You are concerned about your own capability to do things alone.

Is this fear relevant to you and how has it impacted your life?

What could you achieve if this was not a concern to you?

What will you change about how you perceive this barrier?

Be Your Own Hero

You fear starting your life over.

Is this fear relevant to you and how has it impacted your life?

What could you achieve if this was not a concern to you?

What will you change about how you perceive this barrier?

Lesley Van Staveren

You are scared of losing personal wealth.

Is this fear relevant to you and how has it impacted your life?

What could you achieve if this was not a concern to you?

What will you change about how you perceive this barrier?

Be Your Own Hero

You have a fear of failure.

Is this fear relevant to you and how has it impacted your life?

What could you achieve if this was not a concern to you?

What will you change about how you perceive this barrier?

Lesley Van Staveren

You have a fear of change.

Is this a fear relevant to you and how has it impacted your life?

What could you achieve if this was not a concern to you?

What will you change about how you perceive this barrier?

You have a fear of the unknown.

Is this a fear relevant to you and how has it impacted your life?

What could you achieve if this was not a concern to you?

What will you change about how you perceive this barrier?

Let's again take a closer look at these questions and what your answers might mean in relation to being your own hero:

You are scared of what others will think of you.

Throughout life there will always be moments of growth and change, both personally and professionally. You may be bored or frustrated in your job and have a desire to learn more, perhaps wanting to invest in a personal development course to get clear on what drives you. You may even want to enrol in university to undertake studies that could propel you into an industry or career that fulfils you.

People around you may have their own opinions on your life choices if these choices mean something different to what they expect from you. It comes back to the 'herd mentality' that we so often hear about: If you change the status quo of how things are, not everyone will be comfortable.

This is why who you surround yourself with is of paramount importance. Your tribe should not only champion you but also call you out if what you are doing is genuinely not a well thought-out decision.

Have people around you that think differently, who ask you questions that provoke thought, and that you can respectfully disagree with, while still admiring them for their passion and individuality.

There is a very distinct reason that the concern of what others think about you should not hold you back from following the path you know is right for you.

What people comment on and see is nearly always based on their feelings and insecurities about themselves. Sometimes these thoughts may be so deeply ingrained in their being that they will not realise this is where they are coming from.

You will always come up against judgement in your life no matter what you do. Isn't your life and its outcomes more valuable to you as the person living it than a temporary opinion of another individual looking in from the outside?

After my first marriage broke down, one half of my family disowned me completely. My uncle actually wrote me a letter to tell me that I, specifically, am what is wrong with the world and young people today, that is, their inability to commit and stay in a relationship. He added that he never wanted to hear from me again.

Lesley Van Staveren

I was crushed at the time, and it took me a while to process his response. He didn't even ask if I was okay, or try to gain a further understanding. But you know what, that's okay. I understand now that he was going through a devastating period of loss himself. My actions simply were in direct conflict with his life values, so he chose not to build the relationship again when I reached out. But that's up to him.

You can't control how others feel or react. That's up to them, and you have to respect they are making decisions and taking action with the knowledge they have, which is based on their own experience, beliefs and values. That's their right. The choice you have is how you react to other people's behaviour and thoughts as it's never about you. It is typically a reflection of their own feelings at the time.

I once had an ex-partner express disdain for me taking on personal development training, stating it's all just rubbish so I should go and find someone else to talk about that 'crap' with. It hurt at the time as it was voiced by someone I loved. Back then, I viewed it as disregarding my values and interests. However, when I was able to look objectively at the situation, it came back ultimately to his love for me. Deep down, he feared what changes may have come and how that would impact us as a couple.

Maybe you are in a relationship and have been unhappy for a long time, for any number of reasons. If you are concerned about what others may think about you and your relationship and whatever direction is the best outcome for you both, don't be. We are all human and we all have our own challenges to work through. In the bigger picture, it's your business. No one else has a say in what should or shouldn't happen in your relationship.

You are concerned about your own capability to do things alone.

If you are used to sharing duties in the home or in business, it could be intimidating to start taking responsibility for things that are outside of your comfort zone. Having someone to share the load with can be an amazing experience and can add so much benefit to your life from reduced stress to shared knowledge.

However, this is different to holding yourself back from achieving your full potential due to fear. Or if you are staying in a situation that makes you deeply unhappy. This is when you need to break it down and overcome the real internal barrier.

I recognise that all life situations are different. Some of you may be differently abled or have health implications to consider. In this situation, as with many others, assistance may be vital for your well-being and safety. However, in circumstances where you are fully capable of being independent but may be scared of doing things alone, I encourage you to not be.

Sometimes it can certainly be intimidating to think that there is no safety net and that the buck stops with you. I'd like you to adjust your thoughts on this for a moment. By taking full ownership of all the duties you carry out, it not only gives you a sense of pride but also enables you to learn so much more about yourself—and how much you can actually handle by yourself!

In my experience, I held on for too long in a relationship with a man I loved with all my heart. But unfortunately we brought out the worst in each other. After many years, we realised that we are both happier and healthier apart, which is also so much better for our children's wellbeing.

However, I was initially scared of being by myself as I was fearful how I'd cope with three young kids alone, running the household and being a working mother.

But guess what, all of my concerns were unfounded. In my personal situation, I thrived being back in control of my own household and the kids' routines. I enjoy having a nice balance of structure and downtime in my home.

Make no mistake—it is not easier by any means. It's an increased workload and pressure; however, now the feeling and energy that I have the ability to bring into my home is one of calmness and grounding.

Even though I thrive on juggling all responsibilities on my own since my marriage breakdown, I encourage readers to get professional guidance at such major life crossroads as every situation is different. The safety and well-being of all parties must always be the paramount consideration in how you move forward in whichever direction you choose. Professional guidance may enable you to unravel your thoughts and get clarity on the situation you are in at a real and objective level.

Don't hold yourself back though if your barrier is being scared of how much capability you have to handle each area of your life yourself. By the same token, keep your heart open and be willing to accept help; every situation is different, and you don't need to be a martyr for the cause of independence. This is about you and your self-confidence and self-worth . . . not closing yourself off to a rich and fulfilling life.

You fear starting your life over.

Just the thought of starting over can evoke strong conflicting emotions in people. For some it may be fear and for others it may be excitement.

For followers of Tony Robbins, he highlights that one of the six core needs for us as human beings is certainty. So, when we throw into the mix a core need, combined with the fact that we need an element of routine to be grounded . . . the thought of shifting everything we know about our life is bound to raise some big questions for us. But is certainty just an illusion we have created for ourselves?

Please take a moment to think about this: Starting again can raise questions about how you will cope, how you will earn the income you need and how you will survive. Here's the rub though: Nothing in life is ever for certain when you think about it. You can then start to break down the walls of your own making and ask the question: Is holding on to the fear of the unknown more important than the pursuit of happiness and contentment?

As always, I would like to highlight not to shake things up or to disrupt your life in a way that may have a negative impact just for the sake of it.

This section is for those that have a clear decision to make, have explored all options and done the necessary research into their desired path. If you are at the crossroads of starting again, I recommend that you be in an emotionally strong position and are comfortable with a leap of faith. It would also be a bonus if you have developed the resilience to move yourself forward from a position of strength, or that you have the right support network surrounding you.

The more you understand your own individual abilities and value your worth, the more you can be confident that whatever change occurs in your life, you can and will handle it in the best way you know how.

I have started over twice now. We all have different phases in our lives that are part of our story, our own unique path.

My earliest major change was after separating from my first husband in the UK. I was twenty-three when we got married, only six months after my dad had passed away. During that relationship we had some tough experiences including miscarriages and alcohol abuse, which was immensely hard to work through.

We weren't as well suited as we thought, and as a result the inevitable spilt happened after just a couple of years. We then sold the house and a couple of months later my work contract finished. So, there I was with no official home, no relationship, no job! At first I thought to myself, 'Great, you are twenty-six and have stuffed your life up already.' But it's all about perspective, right? I shifted my thinking and realised the world was my oyster! I straight away booked flights to Australia, the country I had dreamed of visiting all my life.

It turned out my ex-husband was flying to Australia as well, so we ended up flying over together. We travelled as friends for a few weeks before saying our final goodbyes and going in separate directions.

Starting over in a new country and getting my own foundations was the best thing that could have happened to me, and I am so grateful for every experience and learning along the way. It's tough being on the other side of the world away from my family but I have built a support network around me that I'm so grateful for. This network cheers me on, and I give my full heart to them. We are there to cushion and support each other through the difficult times. Change can be scary but it can also be liberating and enlightening.

You are scared of losing personal wealth.

Have you ever lain awake at night thinking about money? Worrying about paying the bills or how to achieve financial freedom? Of course you have at some time or another. Our relationship with money and basing our perceived wealth on this form of value is conditioned into us throughout life.

We are all living in an incredibly material world where we place so much perceived value on the house we live in, the car we drive and the size of our bank balance.

But if you define yourself based on the material wealth you have, and that wealth changes, it can be very hard to recover from emotionally.

This is where the constant practice of gratitude and appreciating the true wealth of your family, kids, health and yes . . . of course, your own inner strength, is important.

Life is short and can change in a flash. For example, who could have ever predicted a global pandemic where the entire world was locked down and you weren't allowed to enjoy all of the many things you can tend to take for granted, such as a coffee with a friend or giving someone a great big hug!

We are all passing through this life; our existence on this planet is temporary. It is a very real thing that the material objects or the money we have will come and go. But it is the pure presence and memories we create that will be our lasting imprint.

For me personally in 2020, due to a multitude of devastating circumstances all occurring over the period of a couple of months, I lost everything from my relationship through to having nothing left financially. I had to make the tough choice of walking away from a business and industry I had put my heart and soul into for the last ten years.

But I am a passionate person and very clear about my own worth as a human being. I know that I am not defined by what I have. I was able to logically process that I was watching my life falling away in front of me. Or what I thought of as my life. Don't get me wrong, I have major ups and downs, and for a period of about two months I would spontaneously burst into tears.

But I can also see all of this for what it is: a processing and release.

Through all this I am grateful for the most important things in my life: my three kids. They are the most incredible little people and bring me so much joy.

I am also grateful for my health; I run 2–3 times a week and keep my body moving as well as do daily meditation and stretching.

So I ask you to review your answer about fear of losing personal wealth and change your perspective on what true wealth is to you.

Once you do not have a fear of losing monetary value, you can let go of the negative energy you direct into that type of wealth. This will allow you to move forward in a way that is true to you and gives the space for bringing what you are passionate about into your life.

You have a fear of failure (Atychiphobia).

There are multiple barriers we each place on ourselves, and quite often the perceived fear is more debilitating than what the outcome is in reality. It is more likely that the feelings associated with fear are the real barrier, such as shame, embarrassment, disappointment, regret or frustration.

Lesley Van Staveren

Does the fear of failing bring you to a grinding halt? How you perceive this fear is everything. One of my favourite sayings is, 'There is no failure, only learning.' That is a principle I live by now; in my life I am not afraid to put myself out there or try new things. Because you know what, if it doesn't work the first time, I just make a note of what I would do differently the next time. I don't let that experience go to waste.

If you think that you have failed if something doesn't go to plan, this can cause unfounded and unnecessary anxiety and stress.

Think back to where this fear may have come from. Is it because you have been repeatedly told you can't do something? Or have you had a traumatic event occur in your life?

Or perhaps something didn't go to plan and you felt foolish. A couple of these areas go back to where you seek approval from and what that means for you. This is where being kind to yourself, having positive self-talk and truly having your own back will assist you to venture into areas you didn't think possible and trust in your own abilities.

If you have had a traumatic event that is holding you back, you may have unresolved feelings that would need to be explored with a psychological professional. Our brain is so complex and can bury many things that have been too painful to process by ourselves. It can take someone else with the right skills to unlock this in a healthy and safe way.

If you are scared of failure, you could be missing out on some extraordinary opportunities that can bring great learnings and experiences into your life.

Look at Oprah Winfrey; she was told in her early years she was unfit for TV. Or Walt Disney, who was fired from one of his first jobs for lack of imagination.

We each have a unique gift to share with the world. It is you who has to have faith in yourself. Win or lose, that is the learning that you are meant to experience at that point in time to take you to where you are meant to be.

For me personally I don't believe I have ever failed. That's a big statement, right? No . . . what I believe is I have messed up in life, I have loved and lost, I have had jobs and it hasn't always gone the way I thought, I have taken risks and sometimes it hasn't gone to plan. But every single time I have learned something new and grown as a person.

I ask that you change your language around this. If your fear of failure has come from what someone else has said and made you feel, separate the voices, get clear on where that belief has come from and ask if that is actually from you or if it is someone else's fear that has been projected onto you. If it's is the associated feelings of failure that you are fearful of experiencing, this is why working with learning tools to process negative emotions and having true inner self-worth makes the difference in how you approach situations and opportunities.

It is most often the times that something hasn't turned out how you thought it would that has challenged you to think differently, to be resourceful and creative in a way you may not have thought possible.

Get clear on the worst-case scenario and have a contingency plan. There is no failure . . . only learning.

You have a fear of change (Metathesiophobia).

The fear of change is interconnected with everything I have previously written about: the concern about not being about to cope by yourself, the fear of an unknown outcome and the worry over what people will think.

As humans, it is quite common that we narrate a story in our minds, ruminating about what will happen to us in every situation. Often, it's these made-up scary stories that we listen to most, at the expense of reality.

But what if you could change the story you tell yourself? You see, every single story has an ending. You will land on your feet and find a way through no matter which direction your life heads in.

It is when you doubt your ability to handle what comes with change that you will stop in your tracks. By releasing the need to control everything, you gain control.

The fear of change may come from the knowledge that to move on means you have to close the previous chapter; this can bring so many painful feelings no matter what it is. If you are holding on to a previous relationship because you are living in the story of what you expect it to be in the future, you are not giving yourself permission to accept the reality of the situation. And you won't be able to let go.

If you are stuck in a relationship that you know is not healthy, I suggest you follow the path of guidance and counselling as necessary. It could be that with simple shifts and behaviour change, there can be a great future ahead for that relationship. But if this is not the case and it really is time to close that chapter, sometimes not knowing what lies on the other side can be terrifying. It feels safer to stay where you are because it's what you know. You may be scared of being alone or wondering if you'll ever meet someone again, or you may be scared about how you will cope with all the extra responsibilities.

This is where you need to change your story. You can adapt to any situation, you will find a way to cope and you have all the skills you need to be able to embrace a new way of life. You just need to learn to love you, who you are by yourself, and really get to know you as a person all over again. This is a time to strengthen your appreciation of your own value and capabilities.

Yes, things may be bumpy and painful at the start. Don't think things will be easy, but don't wish that they were. Take on the hurdles that come up as learning points to give yourself more life skills and resilience. Ensure you have a plan and the necessary support network to move forward in whichever direction is the right one for you.

If you have children, this is never an easy decision, and you have to factor in their health, well-being and emotional support. With every considered change, please bear in mind who else may be impacted and if this has any further unintended consequences.

If it is leaving a job you are deeply unhappy in that is the change you are scared of, ask yourself why. What are you settling for and what is the story you are telling yourself? Are you denying yourself finding a role that is more fulfilling? Or is there a different skill you'd like to learn but you doubt your ability to do something different?

You are not defined by your circumstances; you are the one in control of your choices.

As a woman with three young kids who has lost all assets, my relationship, and had everything I know flip on its head, I can confidently reassure you it will be okay. It's not easy, but there is no learning or enrichment in easy. Change can bring spectacular things and opportunities into your life. You just need to perceive the challenging times as a way to propel you ahead to the correct path.

You have a fear of the unknown (Xenophobia).

This fear can be present in so many ways. It can arise from a change in life circumstances through to someone different coming into your group of friends that changes the dynamics and throws you off balance. There is currently research being carried out by Harvard on just how easily xenophobia can be switched on. What they are finding is that within hours, we can be conditioned to discriminate against those who are different to ourselves. How much division is in our world caused by our underlying fear of the unknown?

The reason I open with this is to highlight how susceptible we are if we are not really clear on our values and what we stand for. This applies to all aspects of our lives. I ask you: Do you know how this fear may play out for you in particular and are you aware of any reactions that may stem from xenophobia? We certainly need the protection mode of the brain to keep us safe and to make logical decisions. But problems arise when the fear of a perceived threat or something that may never occur takes over our ability to live a life true to ourselves. When this happens, it becomes harder to step out of our comfort zone.

As an example, someone may be comfortable in a clear swimming pool. But that same person may have challenges swimming in the ocean or a lake as there is a great element of the unknown where they can't see what lies underneath.

This principle could also be applied to your life. If you can always see what's ahead, you know how to deal with it. That is no doubt a great position to be in. But that's not reality. You will be thrown curve balls and you will have situations rise up that you haven't expected and didn't want. That's part and parcel of our existence. Having faith in yourself to show up without fear and take on whatever comes at you means you can begin to learn the tools to navigate any situation.

Past experiences certainly have an impact on how you approach the unknown in a variety of situations.

For me, I have encountered this in many areas of life, just like all of you. There are two scenarios in particular I wish to share. The first is that for a long time, I didn't like anyone getting too close to me. I had lost half of my family by the time I was twenty, and then after that I lost my dad when I was twenty-three, and then my grandmother. People just didn't exist permanently in my life and it hurt. I developed a fear of what may happen if I let someone in fully.

By doing this, I actively chose to subconsciously put barriers in place, not allowing myself to truly feel connection and to be vulnerable with others. But it is the ability to let ourselves go and be vulnerable that allows the most beautiful social connections to form.

My other greatest fear of the unknown was after having three miscarriages. I then developed the unfounded belief that my body couldn't carry children. This was unfounded, but because of my fear of the pain I had felt in the past, and the fact I didn't know any different, it felt real to me. Then during my fourth pregnancy, time went on and I saw my beautiful baby growing. But I had to learn to process any anxiety or depression about losing her each time I experienced these emotions.

These unfounded fears and their accompanying emotions were something I had created for myself, so I had the power to choose how I dealt with my fear of what lay ahead.

There are a complex variety of reasons why we fear the unknown, from past experience, to what we are conditioned to believe as we grow up, and we whether we believe we are able to handle ourselves.

Fortunately, there are many techniques to introduce into our daily life to begin to manage this fear, such as:
- Meditating daily
- Acknowledging our own capabilities
- Identifying the cause of the fear and understanding it
- Questioning the fear....yes, we must call ourselves out on this
- Accepting whatever an outcome may be
- Riding the wave of the fear and embracing the learnings along the way
- Practising mindfulness, gratitude and self-love.

> Each one of these fears links back to one thing: YOU. I encourage you to be accountable for your own capabilities and have faith in yourself.

Understanding Your Body's Responses

Each of us has an internal compass that has evolved over millions of years. Yes . . . you've got it, it's your body. Learning to listen to your body is one of the greatest gifts you can give yourself. Isn't it incredible that so often we dismiss one of our most powerful abilities even in the most important decision-making moments in life?

Developing a sense of intuition and having faith in what your body is telling you is how you will navigate yourself to where you are supposed to be—and reduce your involvement with people or situations that are not healthy for you.

How often have you either said or thought, 'There's something not right but I can't put my finger on it.' Or you have felt something is wrong deep in your heart but have said to yourself you are being ridiculous?

Being present enough to trust what you are feeling enables so many positive outcomes to flow in to your life. These outcomes can include being more in control of your own decisions, grabbing opportunities with both hands that you know are right for you, knowing when something isn't right and being able to ask for help, and sensing when others may be experiencing something difficult but can't verbalise it.

You can trust your inner knowing that you are on the right path. What is meant to be will come in time, empowering you to keep your head up through the hardest times.

Be Your Own Hero

> Let's now explore this in a way that is personal to you. I'd like you to again pause, breathe deeply and take a moment to write down your answers to these questions.

Be Your Own Hero

Throughout your life have you had a common health issue surface in a particular part of your body, like headaches or stomach aches?

Do you pay attention to any immediate body signals/reactions?

If you don't listen to your body, why not?

When have you paid attention to a feeling and acted on it and were grateful for the result?

Do you freely express your emotions?

Do you feel fully present in your life and your body?

Do you feel guilty for creating time for self-care and looking after your body and mind?

Before delving into this chapter further, I'd like to share some of my experiences with you. Please note, however, that where there are serious physical conditions you MUST always seek the appropriate professional advice.

For me, my physical challenge has been my throat for as long as I can remember. As a child, I would always have a throat infection of some kind; I lost count of the amount of times I had tonsillitis. I even had my tonsils out when I was seven but the throat infections kept coming. Every time my body would get run down even up until the present day, the first symptom I would notice is a sore throat then swollen lymph nodes.

In the last few years, I have spent a lot of time focusing on my spiritual journey, and part of this was gaining deeper knowledge of the chakras. I still have much to learn, but during my journey I discovered that the throat chakra is connected with communication and not speaking your truth. When I grew up I was always too scared to speak up as I had a belief that I wasn't good enough and didn't deserve to be heard. No wonder I had throat infections.

Over more recent years, I have developed a sense of self-value and self-worth. It's not arrogance. It is a feeling of having confidence in what I stand for and that what I have to say is relevant and valuable. This is a feeling that every single human being is entitled to. When we each value ourselves from a place of contentment, there is no need for comparison. We can each be secure that our voice deserves to be heard.

To get to this point it takes work and regular self-reflection practice. It's not always pretty and we won't always like who we see. But that's the point; it is the polarity of our personality, all elements of us and the acceptance of our behaviours and actions that grounds us to speak our truth.

I am now clear on my 'WHY', or what I stand for. This is the sustainability of our planet and our respect for each other as human beings. All roles of my life from work, hobbies, and of course, how I treat others, comes back to those two 'WHY's'. This is why I also ask that you be true to yourself and what you believe in.

I encourage you to take the time to pay attention to any regular issues you have. Ensure you always seek medical advice when necessary.

The following section details a variety of common ailments and their connection to each of the seven chakras. For those of you who aren't aware of the chakras, they are wheels of energy throughout the body where consciousness and the physical intersect. I recommend that if any of these ailments regularly occur for you, it is worth noting if any of the associated feelings or symptoms resonate with you. Whether you are ready or not to start looking into the chakra system fully, you will see a common focus in the recommendations on keeping positive energy flowing, being fit and mindful of your health, and connecting with nature. All paths lead to health and a positive mindset, and that is always a good thing.

1st– Root/Base Chakra (red)

The root chakra facilitates our connection to the earth. It represents health, survival, abundance and the ability to move forward in life.

Element: Earth

Common ailments: lower back pain, constipation, diarrhea and issues with groin, hips, legs and feet.

Feelings associated with blockage: Loneliness, ungrounded, depressed, indecisive, lack of confidence.

Recommendations: The root chakra is known for its feminine energy; it is the first of the seven chakras and governs the fight or flight response. The colour associated with it is red, and being the base chakra, it is all about balance and grounding:

- ✓ Connect with the earth by either sitting on the ground and/or connecting with the soil or grass.
- ✓ Get out in nature and walk, taking in deep breaths of fresh air.
- ✓ Practise gratitude for what you have as this develops the appreciation for what is truly precious in this world: the love around you, the social connections you have, family and the air that you breathe.
- ✓ Minimise attachment to material objects. This brings grounding and a sense of security back to you.

✓ Base your decision-making process on trust as opposed to fear.

2nd – Sacral chakra (Orange)

The second chakra is connected to our spirituality, other people, creativity, energy and sexuality. It is located below the navel in the centre of the belly.

Element: Water

Common ailments: Sexual disorders, lack of interest in sex, dysfunctional menstrual cycles, lower back pain.

Feelings associated with blockage: As the sacral chakra is connected to energy, if this is blocked you may feel lethargic and unmotivated. This may show up as lack of interest in sex or exercise, low self-confidence, emotional attachments and dependency issues.

Recommendations: The second chakra is located in the pelvic and hip area so creating a flow of the energy in this area is the key to balance and healing:

- ✓ Practise hip-opening yoga postures to allow better flow of energy.
- ✓ Dancing is all about the release of creativity so get some music on and let yourself be free.
- ✓ Focus on fitness and strength.
- ✓ Acknowledge your sexual creativity and beauty.
- ✓ The element connected to the sacral chakra is water, so ensure you keep hydrated (we all know this is a must for health) but also spend time by rivers, lakes or the ocean.

3rd – Solar Plexus Chakra, located at the diaphragm (Yellow)

This chakra is connected to personal power, gut instinct, desire, warrior energy, self-discipline, identity and inner strength.

Element: Fire

Common ailments: Poor memory, lack of concentration, sugar addictions, irritable bowel syndrome, constipation, acne, issues with pancreas, liver and colon.

Feelings associated with blockage: Powerlessness, stomach pains, anxiety, inability to commit, regular feelings of fear, helplessness, struggling to see the big picture.

Recommendations: The Solar Plexus Chakra is associated with the element of fire so bring this into your practices (in safe ways):

- ✓ Light candles during meditation.
- ✓ Strengthen your core to support the fire in your belly (very relevant analogy for this purpose).
- ✓ Sit by a bonfire.
- ✓ Find reasons to laugh (let's face it, laughing is always good for the soul).
- ✓ Spend time outdoors in the sun.

✓ Practise yoga and incorporate sun salutations and warrior poses for connection to inner strength and the fiery energy of the sun.

4th – Heart Chakra, located in its namesake, the heart (Green)

The heart chakra is associated with love, beauty, compassion, serenity, balance and is said to be the bridge between the physical and the spiritual.

Element: Air.

Common ailments: Poor circulation, conditions associated with the heart and lungs.

Feelings associated with blockage: Manipulative behaviours, unworthiness, lack of trust in yourself, lack of proper personal boundaries, losing sense of identity, giving to others or to causes without boundaries, neglecting self-care, impatience, jealousy, disconnection.

Recommendations: As this is the heart chakra, so much can affect its balance including toxic relationships, grief, loss or difficulty accepting a truth about yourself. As with anything, it is complex and you may need to seek help to process these blockages, but here are some helpful recommendations:

- ✓ Practise a guided heart chakra meditation.
- ✓ Incorporate green into your world.
- ✓ Focus on your breathwork. The element is air so bringing mindfulness to your breathing can have a powerful effect (research the Wim Hoff method).
- ✓ Get out amongst the trees and absorb the energy.
- ✓ Establish personal boundaries.
- ✓ Be aware of your thoughts about other people and ask yourself where they come from.
- ✓ Hug more!
- ✓ Allow yourself to receive love. We are so caught up in giving to others, but being able to receive love and feel worthy of it is just as important.
- ✓ Practise forgiveness.

✓ Stretch your chest, upper back and shoulders.

5th –Throat Chakra, located in its namesake, the throat (light blue/turquoise)

The throat chakra is about self-expression, speaking our truth and our purpose in life. It is centred around communication (both verbal and non-verbal) and is the energy passage between the heart and head.

Element: Sound.

Common ailments: Throat infections, dental issues, mouth ulcers, headaches, neck pain.

Feelings associated with blockage: Lack of connection to life purpose, not listening with intention, fear of speaking, shyness, stubbornness, insecurity, a feeling that others won't be interested in what you have to say, unable to express yourself, a sense that people don't know the real you.

Recommendations:
- ✓ Get clear on your life purpose. What do you believe in and are you staying true to your values?
- ✓ Speak up when you feel something.
- ✓ Acknowledge and release feelings such as guilt and resentment.
- ✓ Get clear on what you want to say and the outcome you want to achieve.
- ✓ Develop the skill of articulating your true feelings.
- ✓ Be honest with yourself and others.
- ✓ Practise a throat chakra meditation as the element associated is sound. Humming can achieve balance.

6th – Third Eye Chakra, located between and slightly above the physical eyes (Indigo)

The third eye links to our intuition, our ideas, the mind and our dreams. It connects our life to the universal plan and the enables dream interpretation. As its element is light, it illuminates everything exactly as it is without our personal filters such as our own values, beliefs and experiences. It is all-seeing and is the energy for spiritual insight and reflection.

Element: Light or extrasensory perception.

Common ailments: Ear problems, difficulty hearing, eye problems, headaches, migraines, hair issues, spinal issues, nightmares, hallucinations.

Feelings associated with blockage: Lack of faith in your future path and your purpose, difficulty making decisions, inability to be aware of gut feeling/instinct, difficulty balancing reason or applying logic, paranoia, feelings of pointlessness or insignificance, difficulty changing your mind.

Recommendations: Balancing the third-eye chakra is connected with gaining clarity, deeper perception, inner wisdom and freeing innovation. This enhances your ability to develop and trust in your own intuition, to learn from the past and have a knowing of the future:

- ✓ Practise a guided third-eye meditation.
- ✓ Ensure you have enough sleep.

- ✓ Aromatherapy.
- ✓ Explore and truly listen to different perspectives.
- ✓ Focus on mindfulness.
- ✓ Identify your limiting beliefs and do the work to achieve release.
- ✓ Reflect on what you believe and why.
- ✓ Write down your dreams and analyse the meaning.

7th – The Crown Chakra , located at the very top of your head (Violet)

The crown chakra is our spiritual connection to the divine, and we may hear this referred to as the thousand-petal lotus. It allows the giving and receiving of the energy of consciousness. It has been described in many forms, so we may be familiar with the crown chakra in the form of our higher self. It is the ability to see wholeness in everything around us and to be physically

and spiritually connected. It facilitates the path to enlightenment.
Element: Thought

Common ailments: Insomnia, depression, chronic fatigue, headaches, delusions, sensitivity to light.

Feelings associated with blockages: lack of compassion, materialistic, boredom, egotistic, brain fog, loneliness, not connected with others, a feeling of meaninglessness, angry at life circumstances, happiness dependent on external conditions.

Recommendations: You may hope to attain immediate connection to the spiritual world but this is a lifetime practice. Part of the beauty of working towards balancing the crown chakra is a feeling of contentment, inner peace and clarity. It is developing a sense of being and connection that allows you to have deep compassion for others, appreciation of the beauty of life, respect for different values, beliefs and the trust that there is a bigger plan meant for you. You are worthy and have a purpose to your existence:

Be Your Own Hero

- ✓ Meditate daily – yes, I mention this in each chakra because this is a vital part of balancing your whole being. Each chakra requires a different focus.
- ✓ Educate yourself and expand your mind.
- ✓ Remove clutter from your space.
- ✓ Be open to guidance. When you see a sign, be aware of it. It could come in the form of a dream, repeating numbers, dreams or coincidences.
- ✓ Experience Sound therapy.
- ✓ Spend time reading in the sun.
- ✓ Use positive affirmations.
- ✓ Practise yoga postures that stabilise the crown. (There are amazing yoga instructors, engage with someone you connect with to develop this skill).
- ✓ Be aware of what you are consuming physically and emotionally. This includes the people you surround yourself with, social media or the news you watch.
- ✓ Keep a gratitude journal.
- ✓ Get involved with volunteer work.

Now, let's again take a closer look at these questions from the beginning of the chapter and what your answers might mean in relation to being your own hero:

Do you pay attention to any immediate body signals/reactions?

It is so easy to dismiss a feeling in the body; we do it all the time. I bet you may even be thinking of a time you did exactly that as you read this sentence. Before you can even begin to pay attention to your body's signals, you need to be aware of how your body responds when it speaks to you. For example is it:

- Goosebumps?
- Cold sweats?
- Hair rising on the back of your neck?
- A sick feeling in the pit of your stomach?
- A sense of deja-vu?
- Your eye twitching?
- Anxiety?
- Sudden exhaustion?

Being present in your body helps you be aware of any changes in how you feel. PAY ATTENTION. This can help steer you clear of toxic people or bad situations.

One of my strongest memories is when I was fifteen. I was a difficult teenager and was out drinking with a girlfriend. We had met up with a couple of older boys and were having a great time with lots of laughs, and then they invited us to go to where they lived. They seemed nice so we went with them. But as we got closer, we saw their home was a few caravans in a dark field, and they indicated for us to crawl through some cut-wire fencing to get there.

My friend and I looked at each other; my skin broke out in a cold sweat, and I felt sick to the stomach.

I said no and that we had to get home, so we turned and left very quickly. The boys didn't try and stop us and let us go with no problem, thankfully. But how often when we are young do we just go along with things because we are worried about someone's reaction if we say no? I look back at that night and don't know what may have happened if we had crawled through the fence into that dark field. Maybe nothing. Maybe it was innocent but my body sure as hell didn't agree, and I was not going to give it a chance to find out otherwise.

If you don't listen to your body, why not?

Do you perhaps think your mind knows best? Are you even connected to your body?

That may sound like a strange thing to ask, but if you aren't listening to your body, it could be because of a whole range of reasons . . . and you may not be aware of any of them. It comes back to being mindful and building self-awareness.

You may have a huge week and a long list of tasks at work or duties at home to wade through. Who has time to stop and listen?

I encourage you to make time as this is your intuition speaking up, your navigation system. If you choose to ignore feelings that come up physically, it can have a number of outcomes.

This can be on the health side of things where you ignore symptoms for way too long and keep pushing past your limit. You then get to a point physically that becomes a really long road back to recover from.

I did this myself a couple of years ago. I ignored the fact I was exhausted, run down, had a fast heartbeat, could hardly breathe and had no ability to remember the simplest things. This was burn-out banging at my door but I kept on pushing, trying to be a good mum, trying to keep up with work and the home and not giving myself a break. I learned my lesson but it took months of recovery.

The other problem is by not listening to the warning signals of your body, you have the potential to get involved in a friendship or partnership that is bad for your health. It ultimately may take away valuable parts of you such as your internal confidence and self-worth.

So please slow down and listen to your body as it is your best friend and your true life partner.

When have you paid attention to a feeling and acted on it and were grateful for the result?

Recognising the beneficial outcome of stopping, listening and acting on your body's responses when making decisions, really assists in building your trust in your intuition. Being your own hero is about having faith in your gut feelings and really knowing yourself.

Doing this can give you life-changing experiences and even precious time with those close to you.

One time that this ability hugely impacted my life is when I was twenty-three. My sister and I had gone to the hospital where our dad was getting test results back. It turned out he had stage four lung cancer, and it was too far advanced to do anything about it. I remember the three of us sitting on the edge of the hospital bed, him in the middle with his arms around us as he broke the news.

After four and a half months, we had watched our handsome, strong dad steadily decline and stayed with him in the hospice as much as possible in his final weeks.

It was at that point we had the conversation with the doctors again about his time left; they believed he still had around three months. My sister and I spoke afterwards as we both had such a strong feeling it would only be about another two weeks. We listened to our gut and didn't leave his side.

In two weeks' time we were there by his side when he fell into a coma and then took his last breath. Listening to my gut gave me more time with a man I adored and that is irreplaceable.

This is a deeply personal example. There are so many other amazing outcomes that I can imagine you may think of, from going for a job you knew was right for you or taking the leap of facing a fear and jumping out of your comfort zone because you had faith in yourself.

Do you freely express your emotions?

We regularly hear the term emotional intelligence in the business world and applaud intuitive leaders. However, this form of intelligence is so relevant at every single stage of your life.

Decades ago, if you were upset or crying you may have been told to toughen up or get over it. We are often conditioned to bottle things up.

It's refreshing in current times to see so much more focus on expressing what you are feeling and thinking. This is a critical skill, starting with our children, so they grow up into being connected adults who can say what they feel, clearly communicating challenges they may be having.

There is an undisputable and proven connection to negative physical effects if you hold feelings inside. Unexpressed healthy emotions can build up into frustration, anger, stress, anxiety and feelings of helplessness. If you aren't in touch with who you are or where your feelings are coming from, you may struggle to even unravel *what* you are feeling.

If you do struggle to express what you feel, I would recommend seeking guidance from a professional to begin to break this down in a bite-size way. This would enable you to gain strength and the ability to regulate your emotions, express yourself and build your internal resilience.

Being able to express what you are feeling in a respectful way can build bridges and strengthen connections with the people around you. It is part of demonstrating vulnerability, which is the beauty of being human.

Do you feel fully present in your life and your body?

Did this question make you stop and think about whether or not you are fully immersed and 'awake' in your life?

As I mentioned earlier in the book, humans have a need for certainty and routine. It creates a sense of security. Because of this, it is very easy to go on auto pilot and the monotony of day-to-day life if you allow the fear of the unknown or lack of faith in your abilities to override your thoughts. You may then fall into habits in relationships, the home, work or even how you interact with your kids or your friends.

No amount of doing can ever create being. When I ask if you are present, I mean do you embrace moments of spontaneity and joy? Do you let go sometimes and give yourself permission to just 'be'?

It is very common to allow the chatter inside your mind to take over. You know the one, the never-ending list on repeat in your head of the things you have to get done.

Don't try to do everything at once; we constantly talk about the ability to multi-task, but you know what? That's exhausting. Allow yourself to do one task at a time then move to the next.

I recommend that you be conscious of what is a priority and bring balance into your life. Be mindful of each day and if the chatter in your mind of 'got to do this, got to do that' starts, ask yourself what really is the worst that can happen if you don't.

Take time to breathe, to go outside and look up at the sky. Have a coffee with a friend just because. Play with your kids and embrace the moment of being truly present with them.

Presence and mindfulness comes back to gratitude for what you have in the moment.

You can do anything, not everything.

There is a very good reason we hear constantly about the importance of being mindful.

Do you feel guilty for creating time for self-care and looking after your body and mind?

If you do, it's time to stop right now! There is so much pressure to achieve on every level but you know what? That is all external messaging and perception. What counts is how you feel. What you know is within your physical and emotional capabilities.

There is the understanding that you can't run on an empty tank, and that is so true. If you are not grounded or healthy in yourself, it will bring you to a grinding halt.

Think of the last time you may have been stressed or run down and you made time for yourself to go for a walk or even a massage. Think how recharged you felt afterwards.

It is vital that you make time to relax and recharge. This is where it's so important to know what really works for you personally; you will always have suggestions from others on what has worked for them, which is fantastic. Take it on board but remember your self-care is exactly that – it's about what gives you release from stress and brings your energy back into positive balance physically, mentally and emotionally.

Give yourself permission to sit on the couch and watch a movie every now and then. Be kind to yourself.

Self-care also comes back to drawing your personal boundaries and being comfortable in saying no to people when you don't want to do something. If they don't like it, it's not your problem, and you should probably ask yourself the question why they have reacted that way.

Self-care is respecting your physical and emotional boundaries and not compromising on that. You can do this in an assertive and positive way that is in line with a place of calmness and simply communicating where you draw the line.

Self-care is not selfish, and it is okay to put your well-being first. This way you can give with a full heart and love in a way that doesn't negatively impact you.

- ✓ Plan time for yourself in your routine.
- ✓ Get enough sleep.
- ✓ Create a 'no' list. Be aware of what you don't like doing or what you no longer wish to do.
- ✓ Eat well.
- ✓ Make time for exercise.
- ✓ Identify what areas of your life need boundaries.

Give yourself permission to love yourself. Be kind to yourself in how you fuel yourself physically and with your self-talk because you deserve respect and are worth it.

Owning Your Personal Power

Having a deep understanding and awareness of your own personal power is what can aid you to get through the hardest times, to keep rising against each challenge. It also allows you to know your capabilities and to give with a full heart and know when to let go.

Your personal power is what anchors you to your inner strength, wisdom and resilience.

You build this through having faith in your abilities, doing what is sometimes really hard, pushing yourself out of your comfort zone and not allowing anything or anyone to make you feel emotionally or mentally powerless.

Throughout the book we have covered having confidence in your own independence, speaking up and not being scared to make your voice heard. You also now are aware that it is you that needs to accept and approve of who you are—no-one else.

Your personal power is constantly nurtured through self-love and respect. This is vital. Knowing you are worth infinite love and are not reliant on external factors for your happiness gives you the strength to set your own personal boundaries and have faith in knowing what is best for you.

Personal power is not about closing off the ability to receive love or help from others. Being able to receive love and accept help is a strength in itself and is all part of being complete and balanced.

Being in a place to receive love in a healthy way will come from what you attract into your life. For example, if you simply don't like doing something or are scared of facing a challenge and get someone else to take charge, you have just given away part of your power to someone else.

If you allow someone else to do something for you that you are perfectly capable of and confident in, you are accepting love from a place of self-value where you appreciate that recognition and contentment doesn't come from external factors. But you also know that you are worth loving, and accepting help is not to fill an empty gap or a need based on an area of weakness.

It can be easy to let others take your power away without you even knowing. Part of this comes down to backing yourself, knowing your boundaries and listening to your own intuition.

It could be your boss, your spouse or a friend. But here's the thing: They may not even be trying to take control in a negative way. There are a lot of amazing people in this world that may simply do something for you from a place of love. But that is not always going to help you; avoiding what is hard does not help you grow.

If you are the type of person who always wants to make others' lives easier, ask the question is that really the case? Or by stopping what they are struggling with, are you taking away their opportunity to learn and grow as a person?

Lesley Van Staveren

A seemingly innocent way of giving your power away is to allow others to run things you don't enjoy. For example, finances. Do you allow your partner to control this because you either don't enjoy numbers or you don't feel you know enough? This is an alarm bell ringing for you to start getting educated.

Being aware of how and where you are giving your power away is the first step to taking it back.

Be Your Own Hero

> Let's now explore this in a way that is personal to you. I'd like you to again pause, breathe deeply and take a moment to write down your answers to these questions.

What don't you enjoy doing that you allow others to do?

Be Your Own Hero

What is connected to your name that you are allowing someone else to control?

What have you not taken ownership of because you didn't have enough self-belief and then you have regretted it?

Lesley Van Staveren

Do you know the difference between allowing someone else to take the lead in an area of your life because it is a complementary skill they have versus their need to control you?

When have you pushed through the initial feelings of thinking you couldn't do something and discovered that it has enriched your life and your ability to manage your own life in all areas?

Let's take a closer look at these questions and what your answers might mean in relation to being your own hero:

What don't you enjoy doing that you allow others to do?

One easy and seemingly innocent way of giving your power away is by allowing another person to take over some areas of your life simply because you don't enjoy them. It's so common. And of course, it's nice to have others do things for you to ease the load of daily duties or pressure at work. As I have mentioned, being able to receive love and assistance from a place of grounding and strength is a necessary balance in life.

The problem arises when you are in a position of weakness, insecurity, lacking faith in your own abilities or fear that there may be a future issue. Allowing others to take control of areas you don't like when you are in a position of weakness is an exchange of energy where you are giving your power away. As it is an exchange of energy, there will be a price to pay further down the line, so what does having power over your own life mean to you?

Earlier in the book we spoke about the financial side of things; some people thrive on budgeting and working through numbers. However, if this is not your strength, I encourage you to find the enjoyment in it and connect it to a value that does motivate you.

I am one of those people; I'm a big-picture person. Numbers are not my favourite thing. Or are they? You see, what I know with every fibre of my being is that those numbers give security, balance and opportunity. By allowing someone else to handle my finances and take control it has meant I entered into a position where things weren't managed as I would have done. And that is 100% on me, not the other person. I allowed them to take control because it seemed easier, but it's not. There was a pay-off further down the line.

Be aware that some people use finances in a relationship to take control over the other person's life. Taking ownership of your finances puts you in a position of strength in your own life.

I now relish taking control of all financials connected to me as that is my opportunity and blueprint to a bright future. By getting clear on numbers it will enable me to do all that I wish to do in life. What is it that you value and how does it connect with taking responsibility for your finances?

A problem could also be your relationship with money itself and how you perceive it. Some people may say money is the root of all evil. But it's not. Money will be used in the way that the person who owns it, values it. For example, look at Oprah Winfrey. She is one of the richest women in the world and has accumulated her wealth through her love of humanity and she consistently gives back.

Where else in your life have you given power away and why? Is it household chores or even what you wear?

How about having your own voice and speaking up? If making your voice heard is something that makes you feel uncomfortable, someone else will then speak on your behalf. I guarantee that if you are not putting your opinions forwards and making your thoughts known, someone else will be.

If you allow things in the home or work to go on in a way that you disagree with, and you don't speak up, you are essentially giving permission for things to remain that way. Don't be afraid to use your voice; you need to speak for yourself and not allow anyone else to speak on your behalf. Your opinion is valid and worth listening to. It's also your power.

Let's again take a closer look at these questions and what your answers might mean in relation to being your own hero:

What is connected to your name that you are allowing someone else to control?

What came up for you with this question? Was it something that you were already aware of? Or something that perhaps you weren't conscious of?

Think of everything connected to you as your own personal IP. Imagine yourself as a business where you need to break down and identify the different components and who is responsible for each part.

Do you rent a property with someone else? Who is responsible for the payments?

Who is the lead communicator? If it's not you, are you clear on any issues or misunderstandings?

As well as what is being controlled, it is also who is communicating in areas connected to you. If you are not across the specifics and have a clear understanding of where things are up to, it may be you putting out fires further down the line.

This can come back to not wanting to rock the boat or disrupt a relationship. But I will say it again: If you have any inkling that things are not as they should be, listen to your body and ROCK THAT BOAT.

Each person has different skill sets, and it is critical that you have your eye on the ball. If you allow someone else to be the main contact for anything that is connected to you, ensure their skill set and strength includes attention to detail and communication.

This will save you a lot of heartache, I can promise you. Communication is my biggest passion; however, in the past I have allowed another person to speak on my behalf. As it turned out, there was substantial miscommunication on many big issues and even worse, no communication on some occasions. It then reflects on me and my name.

In today's world, perception is everything. You need to be the one that is wholly responsible for what is projected in anything associated with you. Your identity is yours, and yours alone.

Lesley Van Staveren

What have you not taken ownership of because you didn't have enough self-belief and you have regretted it?

We have discussed business, finances and relationships, and if this is what comes up for you, what is going to be your next step?

Your own health is something that can slip under the radar. It can be so easy to take on board all the past negative words you have heard about yourself and allow them to manifest. Mainly because you didn't have enough self-worth to acknowledge what was going on, let alone re-enforce the truth that you know deep inside: That you are in control of your own well-being and how you perceive it.

This is where getting clear on how the negative talk you absorb from others plays out in your mind. It's your life and it's on you to choose what you take in and believe about yourself.

I grew up thinking I was not enough, always compared to others, always thinking I had emotional problems. I had a number of relationships where I would hear that there was something wrong with me mentally, so I started to believe it. In one relationship I was told on many occasions I had depression, so I started to believe it and got lower and lower. This impacted my health too as I built a belief in my own mind that if I exercised, I would get sick, so I didn't exercise, and if I did . . . guess what? I got sick. I had so much belief in what other people told me because I didn't value my own worth enough, and it impacted me in every sense and became debilitating.

I honestly couldn't tell you why I have allowed myself as a woman with fire in her belly to take on board so many degrading comments, to the point of looking in the mirror and thinking I am stupid, worthless and why would anyone listen to me.

But that's the point. We give away too much of ourselves to external influences and we listen to the negatives too much. There is a balance though: If someone is sharing something with you that is genuinely an issue you have that may need attention, then please listen and don't just dismiss someone else's opinion. It comes back to being respectful of others and being in a grounded state. That way you will discern the difference between another person trying to bring you down to either gain control or make themselves feel better versus someone that is looking out for you and is a true friend who will call out the hard truths that you need to hear in a respectful way.

In business this is so common as the different roles in a company are intrinsically linked for them to work harmoniously for the whole business. However, if another person is taking the lead in something you strongly disagree with, don't give up your part in it when that self-doubt creeps in on occasion. It is very likely you will kick yourself further down the line if all didn't go to plan and that you were right all along. Then you have to live with the fact that you knew you should have said something. By not speaking up, you actively chose not to have a say.

Do you know the difference between allowing someone else to take the lead in an area of your life because they have a complementary skill versus their need to control you?

As you transition to a stronger position within yourself, be conscious of the growth, the change in how you feel and how you perceive others' behaviours.

When your personal power begins to rise, it's best to allow it to do so with grace and from a place of fulfilment. This is opposed to becoming a person who tries to gain so much control that you close yourself off to receiving assistance, guidance or support. Or even further, stepping over the line and trying to take control of others.

Grace will come from developing presence in the moment, understanding other people's values and beliefs and listening to your gut-instinct.

Here's what it looks like if another person has bad intentions and does not respect you. This may lead to the situation where they have a hold over you or make you feel bad about yourself:

- ✓ Not respecting you when you outline a personal boundary.
- ✓ Not listening when you say no.
- ✓ Never allowing you to speak up.
- ✓ Telling you that they know what is better for you.
- ✓ Making you feel that you need them for survival.
- ✓ Restricting your social connections.
- ✓ Making you think something is your fault.
- ✓ Criticising you for mistakes and making you feel bad.

- ✓ Always expecting something in return if they do something nice for you: 'I make you coffee each morning so you should be grateful.'
- ✓ Accusing you of being over-sensitive if you speak up in your own defence.
- ✓ Intimidating you either with their physical size or their stature in life.
- ✓ Displaying mood changes. They may make big gestures like buying you gifts and making you feel special then the next minute you are treading on eggshells in case you say the wrong thing.
- ✓ Saying they are your biggest supporter but making you feel insignificant.
- ✓ Dominating you, such as taking control of finances or how things have to be done in the home.
- ✓ Giving you a constant feeling in your gut that things aren't right.

There is a big difference in a true partnership where you have one another's best interests at heart and want each other to step into your own light. This is when you can truly raise each other up, champion each other's abilities and grow as a team.

How do you know when you are on the right track and someone has pure intentions at heart when it comes to you:
- ✓ You are listened to and respected when you say no.
- ✓ You treat each other with respect, not contempt.
- ✓ You trust in your gut that this person will not deceive or betray you.
- ✓ They acknowledge how you are feeling, absorb it and listen.
- ✓ They don't try and make you agree with them when you have a different opinion.
- ✓ They give you space and peace when you need it.
- ✓ You feel appreciated for being you.
- ✓ Your ideas are listened to, and they ask you questions to understand more.
- ✓ If you wish to follow a different path or embark on training to grow as a person, they champion you to do so.
- ✓ You can engage in healthy conflict with each other in a way that does not escalate into aggression.
- ✓ Full transparency and honesty is a given.
- ✓ You are okay spending time apart.
- ✓ You are playful with each other.

✓ You each understand that you and you alone are responsible for your own happiness. You are not dependant on the person to be happy.

As with everything, awareness and paying attention to your intuition will enable you to feel what is and isn't right.

When have you pushed through the initial feelings of thinking you couldn't do something and discovered that it has enriched your life and your ability to manage your own life in all areas?

This is empowerment at its finest. It is the moment you have achieved something that you didn't think was possible and realised with your whole being just how capable you are.

It is possible to be so governed by accepting how things are, while also lacking faith in how far your own abilities will stretch, that you are the one who holds yourself back. It may be a fear that stops you pushing out of that comfort zone, but I say grab that fear and stare it in the eye. Understand where it is coming from and take a leap of faith.

This goes back to how you learned and grew as a child. You were curious and weren't ruled

Be Your Own Hero

by self-doubt. You just gave things a go because it was instinct; you just knew it was something you had to do. Think of a child's first steps, they aren't scared. They keep getting up and trying again and again until they get there.

Or what about when you learned to ride a bike? Did your parent hold onto the back then let go when you were peddling away and all the while you thought they were still there so kept going. Then you looked back and discovered they weren't holding on and that you had the ability all the time.

This same ability could now range from taking a leap and embarking on that degree you have always wanted through to releasing yourself from the shackles of playing the victim and allowing a bad experience to rule how you project yourself in life.

It is you and you only who can dictate how you approach life and what you are prepared to accept.

For me it was when I felt ready inside to own my own power. I then released myself from the concern of what others though about how I lived my life. I know myself and know without question that my intent with anything I apply myself to is for the greater good. If people wish to have their own perception on what I do with

Lesley Van Staveren

my life, that's not my problem. It doesn't mean I don't care; I very much am interested in what others think and my intent is always to make others feel heard and acknowledged. But what I accept is that I cannot please everyone no matter what I do so it is best to allow myself to rise up and play with a full heart in my life.

Having this release has enabled me not to feel I have to stay in relationships that aren't right. I also speak up when I know something isn't right and take control of every area of my life.

I ask you to reflect deeply on this question: 'What is stopping you from taking the lead role in your own life and how is this impacting you?'

Owning Your Mistakes

Owning up to mistakes can be a nerve-wracking prospect. There are so many feelings associated with this, from fear of being judged, looking silly and perhaps not even wanting to admit to yourself that something didn't go to plan because of the level of emotional attachment you have. There is a myriad of considerations all wrapped up in simply holding your head high and admitting you did something wrong.

It's not surprising that it's so hard to do though. We are programmed to protect ourselves and that's okay. However, if you have either done something unintentionally that didn't go to plan or you purposefully made a mistake, you are actually giving your power away if you don't summon the courage to own up to it.

We are all human; we aren't supposed to get everything right. And really, how dull would that be! We fail, we fall, we live and we learn. And it's all relative; the bigger your goals and dreams, the more mistakes you make. So, if you want to keep growing and get closer to where you want to be, start building your resilience by owning up every single time and looking at what went wrong and what you would do differently.

——— Be Your Own Hero ———

> Let's now explore this in a way that is personal to you. I'd like you to again pause, breathe deeply and take a moment to write down your answers to these questions:

How do you perceive a mistake?

Be Your Own Hero

Do you know the difference between owning your mistakes and standing your ground?

Do you blame other people when something goes wrong?

Lesley Van Staveren

Do you worry how you will be perceived if you have done something wrong or that didn't go to plan?

Has there ever been a circumstance where you have put your head in the sand? How did that play out?

Has there been a time you have faced something unpleasant that was due to something you did, which then gave you a feeling of learning or control?

Are you aware of any defence mechanisms you have that may make owning up to things difficult for you?

Let's take a closer look at these questions and what your answers might mean in relation to being your own hero:

How do you perceive a mistake?

Do you see making a mistake as a failure? We covered this earlier in the book and something I truly believe is that there is no failure, only learning.

Each second, the unconscious brain's processing abilities is estimated at roughly 11 million pieces of information a second. By contrast, the estimate is that our conscious brain can process about 40 pieces per second. That's a huge gap! So where will your focus and interpretation be when something hasn't gone to plan? It will go where you direct it.

If you perceive a mistake as an experience that re-enforces that you are no good at something or don't have the skill needed to achieve what you want, your brain will keep on filtering all facts that give you extra evidence to support that thought.

This is why I ask you to consider how you view supposed mistakes and even change your internal dialogue completely. If you can begin to see every single 'mistake' as a lesson, you will approach it with an entirely different energy and from a perspective of growth.

Think about growing up. If you touched a hot kettle, I bet you didn't do it again. What about in your first job? Did you know everything or did you stumble across a few hurdles that then enabled you to avoid doing the same thing?

It's a bit like trying to learn a maths equation. If you kept trying to work something out the wrong way, you may keep coming up with the wrong answer. But if you listened to guidance and advice on how to correctly calculate the equation, you would take that on board, right? You haven't failed; you just acknowledge that it could have been done via a more effective method. If you hadn't been open-minded enough to look at doing it a different way, you would never learn and you would keep repeating the same mistake.

Do you know the difference between owning your mistakes and standing your ground?

Throughout the book I have spoken about having a voice and standing your ground. It's a necessary internal awareness to know when you need to own up to a mistake and when you need to stand your ground.

There are so many moments where you need to listen to your intuition and trust your judgement to speak up when you know something is wrong. However, from an equal perspective, you will have a feeling arise when you know it's time to admit you are in the wrong.

It may be something you don't wish to admit to because you are embarrassed or ashamed. Or perhaps because admitting you are wrong to someone else about how you have behaved or how something has turned out, it means you have to do a lot of internal work to overcome a barrier in your own mind first. This is all part of the necessary internal work you need to do to be able to release emotions that are not serving you.

This can result in digging your heels in and making things worse on all levels when you perhaps know deep inside it's time to let go of the story you have created to protect yourself.

I remember being at senior school and called into the office with one of my friends. We had misbehaved but I was so adamant that I wasn't going to accept fault. So I kept arguing my side without giving the respect of listening to the teacher in question or my friend telling me to stop.

I had so much frustration and insecurity in myself that sometimes holding on to being right was the one thing I owned. But here's the thing: I wasn't always right . . . none of us ever are.

If you have the incredible gift of knowing when it's time to own up to a mistake, it gives you so many benefits. These include internal peace, learning and also the ability to stop seeing things only from your perspective. This then allows you to open your eyes and your mind to the fact that every single human being deserves to be listened to and courteously acknowledged if you have done something wrong that negatively impacted them.

This is a leadership quality, knowing the balance between speaking your truth and when you are wrong. It shows courage, compassion and humility.

Do you blame other people when something goes wrong?

Something happened at work but it wasn't your fault . . . it was your colleague's fault because they didn't do something right. Or it's your business that is struggling but it's your team's fault as they aren't doing their jobs correctly. Or your spouse is annoying you and the relationship is breaking down but it's their fault as they won't acknowledge their mistakes.

Sound familiar? Every single one of these is a common feeling, and I can relate. No doubt many of you reading this may also resonate with those statements.

But here's the thing: Every single time you have a thought like this you are literally giving your power away to do anything about the situation. This may sound harsh but everything is your fault and if you do not see it this way, you are giving control of your life to circumstance and other people. I want you to take ownership of what is not working in your life and take your power back.

You will have feelings rise up that associate with everything being your fault, but that is the first step of acknowledgement – learning what feelings have surfaced and why. You can't keep brushing feelings under the carpet and allowing other people's behaviour or capability to rule your life. This is your time on this planet, no one else's.

If the statement resonated with you about something not being right at work due to a colleague, why? Was a job done in a way that you

Be Your Own Hero

disagreed with? Did you make them aware of this? If you don't speak up with your thoughts, people will not know. They are just like you, trying to get by and do their best in this world, including their job. I recommend opening the lines of communication by speaking in a respectful way, allowing for the fact it may be your opinion that may not be right in this circumstance. But at least this will allow for a more collaborative way of working for the future.

What about blaming your team for things not going as they should? That is 100% on your shoulders if you are a leader. If you take on the responsibility to lead a team, it is on you to create a space for those people to feel valued, respected and to have a clear understanding of their role. It is on you to give guidance, to navigate the ship. And if things aren't being done how you'd like, it is you who needs to ask the question: Have you clearly communicated the job's requirements so the other person can understand them? It is the communicator's duty to deliver the message in a way that makes it easy for the other person to comprehend.

And if things still aren't working, you might need to look at your own skill set and identify what areas you need to develop. This is why it is so critical to own it when things aren't going to plan. Because if you don't, you won't then see the areas of development for yourself to flourish into the spectacular individual you have the capacity to be.

And lastly, the relationship side of things. As someone who has now had two marriages, you may think, 'What do you know?' I can tell you for a fact I know when things aren't working and why. I will happily admit I can be spiky and difficult; I also edge into my masculine energies too much. I can openly admit that I am far from perfect and I am equally at fault for any breakdown. It's never just the fault of one person. You each contribute to the whole experience that is a relationship.

But I encourage you to be open and apologise when you know you are in the wrong. By the same token, do not allow yourself to be walked over or made to feel wrong if the other person is unwilling to engage in a frank conversation and also own their faults. It goes both ways.

Keep your heart open and acknowledge the light and the dark in yourself and others—it is this that makes us complete.

Do you worry how you will be perceived if you have done something wrong or that didn't go to plan?

This goes back to our previous point when we covered fears; sometimes it's possible to be debilitated by what other people think. However, if you put barriers in place to owning up to something that didn't go to plan (or to wrongdoing for fear of what other people will think), you take away your own opportunity to learn, grow and enhance your potential internal strength.

People will always form their own opinion, and it's not on you to control that. If you spend your life hiding under a rock and unable to speak up and own your mistakes, you will not learn the lesson that is meant for you, and you are giving extra weight to your fear.

Know this: It is undeniably respected when someone has the courage to admit when they are in the wrong. That is one of the biggest forms of strength you can demonstrate by who you are as a person.

It is also quite possible people will have a feeling when you are not being truthful, and if you continue to either deny your part in something or cover up a mistake, respect will be lost. Just as I say to you, 'Trust your gut', you will have a feeling when something is off or when someone is lying. And the same goes for everyone else. We each have the incredible tool of intuition and need to respect that in each other.

Who is it benefiting by you worrying what someone else thinks? It's certainly not you. Standing up and speaking out when you have done something wrong gives you internal confidence. The more you do it, the easier it becomes until you get to the point of absolutely knowing that this is part of the beauty of being human.

Has there ever been a circumstance where you have put your head in the sand? How did that play out?

I appreciate that sometimes this may be the easy option. The situation in question may simply feel too hard to face and you don't know where to start.

But if you don't face up to what is currently happening and deal with it, it won't go away and it will get worse. If you try and ignore what is happening, you are making the choice to give up your own control over doing anything to resolve it and to move forward. It then may build up into a form of self-doubt, insecurity and a fear of any similar situations that arise in the future. Do you really want to be the one who chooses that path for yourself?

It may be a relationship you are in and you haven't behaved as you should, or perhaps haven't been as truthful as the other person may expect. Then over time it gets too big to then admit to, so you keep trying to ignore it and hope it goes away.

It won't. It will build up and come to a head one way or another. And if it is something you could have been open about a long time ago but chose not to, all trust from the other party will be broken. Once trust is gone, it is very hard to win back.

You have the power to speak up and be transparent because you know what? That is all people ever ask for. I'm sure this is something you expect from others and then would feel disappointed if you have been on the receiving end of deceit.

Putting your head in the sand denotes disrespect and lack of consideration to other people involved in the situation.

The same goes for the workplace. If you have done something wrong and hope the boss or a colleague won't find out, they most likely will further down the line. This will then affect your part in the team and the trust and perception from others. It takes away from the integrity I'm sure you as a person may pride yourself on. We all like to believe we do what is best in every situation.

As I say, it's not always that easy as there are underlying feelings such as fear, pride and ego, which are all impacted when it comes to owning up to mistakes.

But consider this: If you make a promise to yourself to face the hard things and to always admit to mistakes, you are showing strength of character, courage and humility. You are giving yourself the respect you deserve by not holding on to things inside, which can then sometimes be too much to bear. This is a form of self-love as you are giving yourself the chance to learn and grow from the circumstance in question.

Has there been a time you have faced something unpleasant that was due to something you did, which then gave you a feeling of learning or control?

Did someone else get the blame for something you did when you didn't speak up? Have you said something awful about someone else and didn't own up to it? Have you taken an opportunity that was meant for someone else? Or perhaps hidden something from someone that then took away their opportunity to act on it?

Recollect the feeling you had when you faced up to something you really didn't want to. This gives you the knowledge and lived experience that if you have faced up to something difficult, you can do it again and again.

You may have memories of letting someone else take the blame for something you did as a child because it felt easier at the time. This may have also set a precedent for the future. Maybe you were allowed to get away with things as child and you could do no wrong? The challenge with this is it doesn't set in place healthy respect for what is and isn't acceptable.

If you have allowed another person to take the blame and never spoken up, did you have a niggling feeling that just wouldn't go away until you made things right?

Your easy option isn't always the right one; that is not where the learning point is. This is why developing your inner strength is key—it empowers you to take things in your stride and take ownership.

How about saying something bad about another person? This is something we are all guilty of, but that doesn't make it okay though. What you need is to be constantly aware of your thoughts about others and how you speak about them. As I mentioned before, it comes back to what feeling another person creates in you and why. Perhaps they are doing something irritating that you just can't stand so you need to have a vent about it? Perhaps someone won something that you wanted or you think they are too big for their boots?

Ask yourself why you are feeling this way, and what does it mean to you personally that they are doing something you want to do? It could come down to aspects you personally need to work on for your own contentment.

To champion another person in their moment of glory is acceptance at its finest as we each deserve our moment in the spotlight. Someone else doing well is something you should want to happen; their light shining does not dim yours. You are an incredible human being in yourself and have a unique gift to bring to the world.

So with this in mind, if you haven't been fair to someone, own it. Speak to them and admit where it came from. This releases you from a weight you may not have realised you had. As I said previously, if you have a negative feeling about someone, it is very likely they will have already felt it. Be the bigger person, own up to your mistakes and apologise for the impact your actions may have had on someone when it is appropriate to do so.

If a situation surfaced in your mind relating to hiding something from someone and taking away someone else's opportunity to act on it, did you tell them in the end? Or did they have to keep on uncovering the fallout from it?

This has happened to me and I can tell you now, I would have been eternally grateful if the other person had been honest at the beginning. When you are in any kind of relationship with someone and you have the choice not to be wholly open about everything, this becomes a betrayal that could have been avoided.

For me, I got to the point where I could have had an impact on the issue in question at the very beginning, but that opportunity was taken away from me. It wasn't as a form of malice; the other person thought they were doing the right thing and protecting me. But this is a perspective I ask that you bear in mind: Even if your intent is to protect or help, if you are withholding the truth and choosing to take away someone else's power in any way, shape or form, this is not okay.

Positives can be taken from every single experience if you choose to be open and see mistakes or wrongdoings for what they are: opportunities to experience life in every way possible. They are also a moment of growth and connection, as well as a path to actually deepen bonds by showing you have the strength at your core to always face the truth. It will give others certainty and faith in you as a person and demonstrates in action that you always act with integrity no matter what.

Are you aware of any defence mechanisms you have that may make owning up to things difficult for you?

Being aware of what shows up for you is the first step to facing every single situation no matter what it is.

Keep revisiting this and make a note of any memories that pop up for you of a time where you have kept quiet and couldn't own up to something.

Factors to consider

Your beliefs about internal change: If you are set in the belief that you personally cannot change, this may limit your ability to own up to your mistakes. Believing you can change is the driver for owning up to things as you will realise you can learn and grow from what occurred.

You feel failure is weakness: If this is a feeling that comes up for you, it may be hard for you to own up to things until you have accepted that it is actually a strength.

You don't value truth: Most people like to believe they value truth, but sometimes the need to be right overpowers being honest. The person may then have their own internal story that re-enforces their 'truth' and that is what they will tell themselves. Here's a red flag though: If you are hearing the same thing from multiple sources ask yourself what would be the worst that could happen by considering their perspective for a moment.

What other people think: Go back to the previous point about other people's perceptions in this chapter as there is always a bigger picture. Don't let things go on for so long that it's now all too hard. Remember, the longer things go on for, the worse they will be.

Admitting you are wrong means making yourself vulnerable: Being vulnerable is a raw

Lesley Van Staveren

beauty that when shown can evoke deep connection with others and internal growth. But because opening yourself up in this way exposes you to the possibility of being hurt, you might put blockages in place to avoid this feeling. Building your self-confidence and self-value aids this as it allows you to open up with the knowledge that you can handle the consequences no matter what they may be.

Self-Acceptance

Self-acceptance is not a default state. How incredible would it be if it were? But then if it were, there would be none of the learnings along the way that give you the understanding of every single element about you as a person.

Self-acceptance isn't just about liking the perceived good parts of yourself. It's the full acceptance of every single part of your personality no matter what. It is the understanding of how you respond in situations, your strengths and your weaknesses.

It is accepting that perfection does not exist in a traditional sense. Perfection is the imperfect, the rawness of humanity, the feelings and emotions that live deep within you. It is also the love of each part of your body and acceptance and love for the way in which it looks and functions.

Self-acceptance is different to self-esteem. Self-esteem denotes how valuable or worthy you perceive yourself to be, whereas self-acceptance is contentment and acknowledgement of who you are. You have no need to prove yourself or shout out your identity, you are simply who you are and that is enough.

For many of my younger years I struggled with this, as many of you reading this may have too. I didn't like who I looked at in the mirror, and I constantly changed jobs as I was always bored. I was kicked out of home at seventeen and then stayed in one different place after another. I believed if I could just meet the right person my life would be okay. Maybe then I would like myself.

But what I now know with certainty is this: I am who I am. No one else can influence that; it doesn't matter where I live, where I work or who I am in a relationship with. I realised no matter what changed externally, I couldn't escape myself, and nor should I want to.

For you, it is knowing that you will go through times of inner peace and contentment

Be Your Own Hero

with yourself to feeling like you are starting all over again. Once you achieve that feeling, it becomes a regular practice that is not guaranteed or perfect. It is you who has to take ownership and responsibility of how you feel about who you are, no one else.

 Be Your Own Hero

> Let's now explore this in a way that is personal to you. I'd like you to again pause, breathe deeply and take a moment to write down your answers to these questions:

How do you feel about your current circumstances?

Lesley Van Staveren

Are you content with the person that you are? Do you acknowledge all parts of you?

Do you embrace the good and bad as all part of your journey?

Be Your Own Hero

If you aren't content right now with your life, where else is it you think you should be?

Do you acknowledge all parts of you?

Lesley Van Staveren

Let's take a last look at these questions and what your answers might mean in relation to being your own hero:

How do you feel about your current circumstances?

Do you define yourself by where you live or your bank balance? What about the clothes you wear or the car you drive?

Do you judge yourself?

These are all external factors, and you are not defined by anything external in this world or any material possession. Of course, it's nice to have these things but that is all a perceived sense of security. Is it real? No. It is the meaning you attach to it.

By knowing that no matter where you are or what you have, you can rise with strength and still love and accept who you are.

I can say this with confidence. I have shared my first experience of starting all over again when I moved to Australia, but the second time is right now.

I live my life with a full heart. I invested everything I had into a business that long-term had the capability to transform regional economies by utilising plastic in a way that can keep capturing what is in existence. But as I mentioned earlier, COVID-19 hit and no-one could have possibly predicted the devastating impact of this. Many of you may have had a similar experience of life-altering circumstances.

I may have lost everything and had to start my life again, but I am okay with that. It wasn't nice to experience and was an emotional rollercoaster without question. But what I knew deep down is that none of that changed me or who I am. I am not defined by my circumstances and neither are you.

I believe during this time, everything that was not meant to be in my life was purged in one go so I could move toward my true-life path. It is my inner dialogue that now empowers me to keep my head up and continue to move forward with love and grace, appreciating that the best outcome and long-term vision is the happiness of my children, while I continue to be the best person I can be, day after day.

Each one of you will have your own story to share and every single experience is relevant and will contain a learning.

Acceptance comes from the inner work, your contentment and the acknowledgement of who you are.

Lesley Van Staveren

Are you content with the person that you are? Do you acknowledge all parts of you?

Do you feel satisfied with the person you are? Do you acknowledge each part of yourself? The light and the dark is what makes you, well, you. As with everything, it is the polarity that gives balance.

You are the only person who can come to this realisation. If you are constantly waiting for something to happen to make yourself a better person, you will always be waiting.

Every single part of you is exquisite and you are made how you are for a very specific reason. There is no one else in the world like you.

But to get to this point, you need to take a good, long look at yourself and that takes strength. You may not be comfortable at first if there are aspects about how you look or about your personality that you have tried to deny and hide. But these are still parts of you.

You need to look at your whole self and make a list of everything you love about yourself and everything you don't like. For what you have noted that you love, I ask that you go one step further and write the reasons why. If this brings up a feeling of discomfort, then look at why. Are you okay with receiving praise and do you truly love yourself as much as you say?

With the parts you don't like, write down why not. To come to a place of acceptance, you will need to go through processing the elements of who you are or what you look like that you don't like. There may be feelings lying deep underneath that need to be unravelled first as we humans are deeply complex. Ensure if you have experienced trauma or may have underlying concerns that you seek the necessary professional help to guide you through this process. Where I say it is you alone that can accept who you are, you may need specialist guidance to help you to navigate through this and unlock certain beliefs.

By coming to a place of knowledge of what drives you, what you believe in, what you stand for and all your unique characteristics, it brings you to a place of inner contentment. This is where your understanding of your self-worth and the value you emit is priceless.

Each part of you is exactly who you are meant to be, and there is never any need for comparison with anyone else. You are a gift to the world in your uniqueness.

Lesley Van Staveren

Do you embrace the good and bad as all part of your journey?

Part of being human is experiencing everything that life throws at you along the way – the highs and the lows. It won't all feel great, there will be pain, loss, grief and a whole lot of other experiences you may have wished hadn't happened. But this is part of what makes you, well, you.

Every single experience and challenge you have encountered through life makes you who you are, from the people you have loved and that are no longer with you, to when you have been on the receiving end of negative treatment from someone else. Sometimes in life the unthinkable happens. It doesn't mean it's okay. Sometimes things happen without us knowing or being able to understand why. The sentence, 'It is what it is,' just sums this up.

There will be pain, but by accepting whatever you have been through and understanding you will be okay and that the sun will shine again, you will get through.

We get thrown curveballs, but equally we have the gift of living and experiencing love, joy, laughter and friendship.

The human experience is messy at times with sometimes no explanation. But spending time in the present moment and accepting everything that comes at you is a learning. It also gives you further understanding of the type of person you are. It allows you to gain a deeper understanding of how you respond, and often you can handle situations that you never thought possible.

Embrace every part of your life; it is your experience. Make your responses and reactions what you choose to have control over. What is within you is what you have ownership of.

If you aren't content right now with your life, where else is it you think you should be?

You are exactly where you are meant to be. If it's somewhere you don't like, why not? What can you do to change that?

If you believe your life isn't what it should be, you are giving away power to what is external to you. If you are frustrated how things have turned out, it may be self-perpetuating. Self-acceptance comes back to the internal. Where else do you think you should be and why?

Do you have thoughts such as, 'This isn't how things should be?' If you do, this will reduce your ability to step up and take ownership of all the elements that we have covered.

If you are where you believe you are meant to be, fantastic. Acknowledge and appreciate it. It is entirely possible to be grateful for having enrichment in your life and being humble all at once.

When you accept yourself it will bring a sense of calmness to you, as well as gratitude for all you are and all you have.

It allows compassion for others around you to flow, to just simply 'be', to listen without judgement and to go about daily tasks with appreciation.

Allow the different energies and experiences to flow through you. When others are experiencing challenge or uncertainty, you can give reassurance from a place of grounding and provide a non-judgemental ear. Being fully content in yourself puts you in a beautiful place where you can put your own opinions and experiences aside and truly listen to another human being from their perspective.

Do you acknowledge all parts of you?

Every single experience in your life, every single relationship and every single duty in your routine is part of you. It is how you approach it all that matters. I recommend that you:

- Live your life with full heart.
- Contribute to others.
- Honour your body and mind.
- Have patience with yourself and others.
- Acknowledge all parts of yourself.
- Own your mistakes.
- Be confident and have faith in your capabilities.
- Know your worth.
- Draw your personal boundaries and do not compromise.
- Face challenges that come up.
- Take responsibility for each area of your life.
- Let yourself be loved.
- Be kind to yourself.

Lesley Van Staveren

Listen to your body; your intuition is a highly developed tool that can guide you through the most difficult circumstances.

You have the ability within you to access what you need to.

Listen to your voice. You are the one who is always there. You are your own champion. You have one life, and it is yours to make it what you choose.

Be Your Own Hero.

ABOUT THE AUTHOR

Lesley Van Staveren was born and raised in greater London but emigrated to Cairns, Australia in 2007. She has three young children, and her vision is to contribute to a socially and environmentally conscious world for future generations to thrive in.

She began her career within recruitment and business development then transitioned to working within the plastic industry for ten years. This included co-founding the first recycled manufacturing facility in Far North Queensland. Lesley is an advocate for the growth of women in manufacturing, driving the development of

Lesley Van Staveren

this in the industry to provide a stronger local economy. She also provides regional entrepreneurship mentoring support.

Being a respected powerhouse within the Cairns community, she actively educates individuals and organisations on plastic, recycling and waste reduction. She has also proactively raised funds for Ruth's Women's Shelter, COUCH, The Junction Clubhouse and Wheels of Wellness. Lesley is also an advocate for female self-empowerment and resilience, and has hosted the 2018 and 2019 and 2020 conference 'Radiance – Illuminating the Strength Within'.

Lesley has always been deeply fascinated by human behaviour. She believes humanity can do so much better as a whole when we enable others to rise, while also appreciating our unique individual value.

She is now an NLP Master practitioner, internal transformation speaker and communication development coach.

Enjoyed the book? You can follow Lesley Van Staveren at:

Website: www.lesleyvanstaveren.com.au

Facebook: www.facebook.com/lesleyvanstav

YouTube:
https://www.youtube.com/channel/UC5KPT1W8d6kwsGUg5FJg7Xg/videos?view_as=subscriber

LinkedIn:
https://www.linkedin.com/in/lesleyvanstaveren/

www.ingramcontent.com/pod-product-compliance
Lightning Source LLC
Chambersburg PA
CBHW010244010526
44107CB00061B/2667